HERO'S WELCOME

by Alan Ayckbourn

samuelfrench.co.uk

FOR AMATEUR PRODUCTION ENQUIRIES

UNITED KINGDOM AND WORLD
EXCLUDING NORTH AMERICA
plays@samuelfrench.co.uk
020 7255 4302/01

Each title is subject to availability from Samuel French,
depending upon country of performance.

THINKING ABOUT PERFORMING A SHOW?

There are thousands of plays and musicals available to perform from Samuel French right now, and applying for a licence is easier and more affordable than you might think

From classic plays to brand new musicals, from monologues to epic dramas, there are shows for everyone.

Plays and musicals are protected by copyright law, so if you want to perform them, the first thing you'll need is a licence. This simple process helps support the playwright by ensuring they get paid for their work and means that you'll have the documents you need to stage the show in public.

Not all our shows are available to perform all the time, so it's important to check and apply for a licence before you start rehearsals or commit to doing the show.

LEARN MORE & FIND THOUSANDS OF SHOWS

Browse our full range of plays and musicals, and find out more about how to license a show

www.samuelfrench.co.uk/perform

Talk to the friendly experts in our Licensing team for advice on choosing a show and help with licensing

plays@samuelfrench.co.uk   020 7387 9373

Acting Editions
BORN TO PERFORM

Playscripts designed from the ground up to work the way you do in rehearsal, performance and study

---

Larger, clearer text for easier reading

Wider margins for notes

Performance features such as character and props lists, sound and lighting cues, and more

---

+ CHOOSE A SIZE AND STYLE TO SUIT YOU

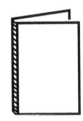

STANDARD EDITION

Our regular paperback book at our regular size

SPIRAL-BOUND EDITION

The same size as the Standard Edition, but with a sturdy, easy-to-fold, easy-to-hold spiral-bound spine

LARGE EDITION

A4 size and spiral bound, with larger text and a blank page for notes opposite every page of text – perfect for technical and directing use

LEARN MORE | **samuelfrench.co.uk/actingeditions**

**Other plays by ALAN AYCKBOURN
published and licensed by Samuel French**

Absent Friends

Arrivals and Departures

A Small Family Business

Awaking Beauty

Bedroom Farce

Body Language

Callisto 5

The Champion of Paribanou

A Chorus of Disapproval

Comic Potential

Communicating Doors

Confusions

A Cut in the Rates

Dreams from a Summer House

Drowning on Dry Land

Ernie's Incredible Illucinations

This Is Where We Came In

Time and Time Again

Time of My Life

Tons of Money (revised)

Way Upstream

Wildest Dreams

Wolf at the Door

Woman in Mind

A Word from Our Sponsor

**Other plays by ALAN AYCKBOURN
licensed by Samuel French**

The Boy Who Fell Into a Book

Invisible Friends

The Jollies

Orvin – Champion of Champions

Surprises

Whenever

**FIND PERFECT PLAYS TO PERFORM AT
www.samuelfrench.co.uk/perform**

ABOUT THE AUTHOR

Alan Ayckbourn has worked in theatre as a playwright and director for over fifty years, rarely if ever tempted by television or film, which perhaps explains why he continues to be so prolific. To date he has written more than eighty plays, many one act plays and a large amount of work for the younger audience. His work has been translated into over thirty-five languages, is performed on stage and television throughout the world and has won countless awards.

Major successes include: *Relatively Speaking, How the Other Half Loves, Absurd Person Singular, Bedroom Farce, A Chorus of Disapproval,* and *The Norman Conquests*. In recent years, there have been revivals of *Season's Greetings* and *A Small Family Business* at the National Theatre; in the West End *Absent Friends, A Chorus of Disapproval, Relatively Speaking* and *How the Other Half Loves*; and at Chichester Festival Theatre, major revivals of *Way Upstream* in 2015, and *The Norman Conquests* in 2017.

Artistic Director of the Stephen Joseph theatre from 1972–2009, where almost all his plays have been first staged, he continues to direct his latest new work there. He has been inducted into American Theater's Hall of Fame, received the 2010 Critics' Circle Award for Services to the Arts and became the first British playwright to receive both Olivier and Tony Special Lifetime Achievement Awards. He was knighted in 1997 for services to the theatre.

Image credit: Andrew Higgins.

AUTHOR'S NOTE

Baba's native language is fictitious and is pronounced very much as written. She comes from a country currently steeped in conflict which deliberately has no specific location.

MUSIC USE NOTE

Licensees are solely responsible for obtaining formal written permission from copyright owners to use copyrighted music in the performance of this play and are strongly cautioned to do so. If no such permission is obtained by the licensee, then the licensee must use only original music that the licensee owns and controls. Licensees are solely responsible and liable for all music clearances and shall indemnify the copyright owners of the play(s) and their licensing agent, Samuel French, against any costs, expenses, losses and liabilities arising from the use of music by licensees. Please contact the appropriate music licensing authority in your territory for the rights to any incidental music.

IMPORTANT BILLING AND CREDIT REQUIREMENTS

If you have obtained performance rights to this title, please refer to your licensing agreement for important billing and credit requirements.

HERO'S WELCOME

First presented at the Stephen Joseph Theatre, Scarborough, on 8 September 2015, with the following cast:

Murray Richard Stacey
Baba Terenia Edwards
Brad Stephen Billington
Kara / Simone Emma Manton
Derek Russell Dixon
Alice Elizabeth Boag
Interviewer 1 Harry Gration (voice only)
Interviewer 2 Amy Garcia (voice only)

Director Alan Ayckbourn
Design Michael Holt
Lighting Jason Taylor

This production began a UK tour at the Yvonne Arnaud Theatre, Guildford, on 13 January 2016.
The role of Baba was played by Evelyn Hoskins, who continued in the role when it was presented at 59E59 Theaters, New York, as part of the Brits Off Broadway Festival, commencing 26 May 2016. Charlotte Harwood also joined the New York production in the role of Kara/Simone.

CHARACTERS

MURRAY – a former soldier, 38
BABA (Madrababacascabuna) – his wife, 22

BRAD – a farmer and landowner, 38
*KARA – his wife, 35
*SIMMY (SIMONE) – their daughter, 17

DEREK – a builder, 43
ALICE – his wife, 39

Two TV interviewers (voices only)

*played by the same actor

SETTING

A bedroom, a kitchen and a sitting room in different
locations.

TIME

A week or so in summer. Any day now.

ACT I

Scene One

As the house lights fade to blackout, the sounds of a triumphal parade with a band and cheering crowd. Over this, as it fades, we hear an INTERVIEWER's *voice.*

INT 1 *(male)* The scenes earlier today in the centre of Hadforth as the town turns out in strength to welcome home, after seventeen years, its very own local hero.

INT 2 *(female)* And now, live from our Hadforth studio we have the man himself, Murray Truscott...

The lights come up to reveal MURRAY *and* BABA *sitting in a remote TV studio side-by-side on a sofa.* MURRAY *is a soldier in his late thirties. He is dressed smartly in his dress uniform.* BABA, *his young wife, in her early twenties, clings to him shyly as if for protection.*

Watching them from home, on her (unseen) wall-mounted TV is ALICE, *late thirties, soberly dressed, seated at the table in her kitchen working on her mobile tablet, only occasionally glancing up at the TV.*

The kitchen, which she shares with her husband DEREK, *is part of their upstairs town centre apartment. One door leads to the rest of the flat. The room has a window which looks straight out on to the precinct below. A table and two stools. At one side of the room, somewhat incongruously, part of an extensive model railway is visible. The bit which we can see emerges from a tunnel to a small station. The line then continues on, stops briefly at a set of operating signals, currently at red and, as*

*they turn green, finally disappears into another stretch
of tunnel. In the living room area,* KARA, *mid-thirties,
sits on her sofa with a cup of coffee, watching her larger
(also unseen) TV. The room is part of her and* BRAD's
*expensively converted manor house. A door to the rest
of the house. A wall of windows with a door leading
directly out into extensive gardens.*

Murray, welcome to Outlook East.

MURRAY Thank you, Judith. Great to be here.

INT 2 Now, before we go any further, I must of course introduce
viewers to your wife – Now it's Madra – I'm afraid you're
going to have to help me out here – Mad – Madra – ba –

MURRAY Madrababacascabuna –

INT 2 Madrababa –

MURRAY – cascabuna... But she usually answers to Baba.

INT 1 *(laughing)* Thank goodness for that –

INT 2 *(laughing)* Yes, I noticed you left that one to me as usual,
Jim...

INT 1 *(laughing)* You know me, Judith, always ready to avoid
a challenge...

INT 2 *(laughing)* Yes, thanks, Jim. Baba – if I may call you
Baba –?

BABA *smiles in response.*

– also welcome. I'm told your wife speaks very little English,
Murray?

MURRAY Not very much at present. But she's learning fast,
aren't you? – *(To* BABA*) Ni cognasca Anglish, Baba?*

BABA *Ni. (Smiling and gesturing a tiny amount) Miniscillee...*

INT 1 Murray, we've just been seeing a recording of your civic
welcome in Hadforth earlier today. That must have been
quite an experience?

MURRAY Yes, it was, Jim. A bit overwhelming. Didn't quite expect that.

INT 1 I don't think the town's seen anything like that since Albion got promoted.

INT 2 According to official figures, a crowd of nearly three thousand...

INT 1 Murray, take us back, if you will, six months or so, to when this all happened. Could you tell us, in your own words, the sequence of events leading up to – what can only be described as an incredible act of heroism. Can you talk us through it, please?

MURRAY Yes, well – we were – me and the rest of the lads – we were – engaged in street fighting against the rebels, you know – house to house –

INT 1 This was you and the rest of your platoon?

MURRAY Yes, largely – and we got – you know – pinned down by these two snipers at high level – pinning us down, like – you know – they were high up on this scaffolding, on the front of this building, this kiddies' hospital – they were really dug in –

INT 1 The building was a children's hospital –?

MURRAY Yes, so we found out –

INT 1 Which the snipers were using virtually as a shield?

MURRAY Right. We couldn't properly engage them, you see. We couldn't call up any of our heavy stuff, even if we'd wanted to, 'cos we were frightened of injuring the kiddies inside...

INT 1 In other words, it was something of a stalemate between you?

MURRAY Yes, for several hours, it was. We couldn't move and they certainly weren't coming down. So we thought, nothing else for it but climb up and try to dislodge them.

INT 1 Which you volunteered to do?

MURRAY *(laughing)* I think I was the only one daft enough. We were just sitting there, otherwise. So I worked my way round the back of them – you know – bit by bit – around to the base of this scaffolding.

INT 1 Which you then started to climb?

MURRAY Well, I started to try to. Only the structure wasn't that stable, you see. They'd taken away some of the main supports low down to prevent us from doing just that. So it was quite hard – and – I must have – you know, as I was trying to get a handhold, I must have – upset the balance of it, its structural integrity, like – and before I knew it, the whole lot came down.

INT 2 You're lucky to be alive...

MURRAY Yes. I had a lucky fall. Sideways into this alcove, like. Protected me. Which was more than it did for them. Eighty foot drop, you know. Both killed outright. Which then left us, you know, clear to enter the hospital building. Where we came under fire from inside. There were more of them inside, waiting for us. Which is when I got the leg injury. So we engaged them, returned fire. Then, once we'd secured the building, made it safe, we realised that meanwhile they'd set fire to it. Smoke everywhere. And then we heard these kiddies screaming. Down in the basement. They'd been locked in the basement. About forty of them. So we set about trying to bring them out, you know. Till eventually there was that much smoke, it became impossible. Then we had to give up.

INT 2 But the point is, surely, Murray, long after your colleagues had given up, you refused to, didn't you? You alone kept going back in to that burning building, time after time, at considerable risk to yourself? After the rest of them had given up even trying? What drove you to do that, do you think? To perform such an amazing act of heroism?

MURRAY *(awkwardly)* Well, you don't really think about it, do you? Not at the time. I don't know. I've been asking myself that. I just felt I – just felt I had to. I just had to. I don't know, really...

INT 1 Well, it's largely thanks to you, that thirty four out of those forty young children, some of them as young as five, are still alive today.

MURRAY Only wish I'd rescued them all, that's all.

INT 2 Well, you would have carried on trying but for your colleagues preventing you. Literally, physically holding you back. That was above the call of duty surely? The action of a hero?

MURRAY *(embarrassed)* I just don't see it like that, you know.

INT 1 Well, there is no doubt in my mind, Murray – I can see you're a naturally modest chap – and I've no wish to embarrass you further but it's an honour and a privilege to talk to you, mate.

In her living room, KARA *reacts.*

KARA *(heartfelt and a little tearful)* Hear! Hear!

INT 2 A truly uplifting story, and a welcome spark of light amidst the appalling darkness of that dreadful conflict.

INT 1 Now, Murray, before we finish, mate. Now, tell me, it's been seventeen years. Seventeen years you've been away. How's it feel to be back?

MURRAY Oh, tremendous. A great feeling, Jim. I'm over the moon to be back here. We both are, aren't we? *(He smiles at* BABA*)*

INT 1 Because, let's be honest – I don't quite know how to put this – but, frankly, you did leave under a bit of a cloud, didn't you? Be honest.

MURRAY Oh, yes well...back in those days I was a bit of – you know –

INT 2 A bit of a tearaway?

MURRAY Yes, you could say that...

INT 1 Well, I'm sure at that age, there are very few of us who wouldn't want people to overlook – how shall I put it – one or two youthful indiscretions –

INT 2 *(playfully)* Speak for yourself, Jim Wilson!

INT 1 – and I'm certain that everyone concerned, after all these years, will long ago have forgiven and forgotten –

ALICE, *alone in her kitchen, reacts.*

ALICE *(dryly)* Ha-ha-ha!

INT 2 So, Murray, tell us about your plans for the future. Is this just a flying visit? Or are you planning on staying here?

MURRAY Oh, staying. We're definitely planning to settle here. I promised Baba, when I married her, I promised to treat her to a little bit of heaven. I promised her the best. In my opinion you can't get better than here. I can't say too much at the moment – but let's just say we've got plans.

INT 1 Can't you tell us a little bit more?

MURRAY No, as I say – I may have left – as you put it, under a bit of a cloud – but I'm determined, you know, to set things straight. And that means, as far as I'm concerned, starting with my mum and dad. My mother, as you may know, sadly passed away a few years back. In fact, that's the only time I've been back here, you know, for the funeral. Compassionate leave. But yesterday I went straight to visit my dad in the nursing home and I outlined my plans to him and he seemed – I'm not sure he was able to take them all in – he's a bit frail these days – but he seemed, so far as we could tell, he appeared very excited by them. So what do they say? Watch this space. Never fear, we're home for good this time!

INT 1 Home is the hero. I'm sure everyone is delighted to see you back.

MURRAY Thank you.

INT 2 And finally, may I put one question to Baba? I know she's been here only a very short while but I wondered what are her impressions so far? I appreciate her English is not very good but does she have one word in English which best sums up her feelings at this time?

MURRAY *(to* **BABA***) Chesta sentimentagies? Instament? Doos? At Anglish?*

BABA *Mees? At Anglish?*

MURRAY *Doos?*

BABA *(into camera, hesitatingly)* He – iss – my – hero.

She smiles and clings to **MURRAY** *tightly.*

INT 1
INT 2 } (touched by this) Ah!

KARA *(likewise)* Oh, that's so sweet! Lovely!

ALICE *(angrily)* Oh, for God's sake! What utter bullshit!

ALICE *irritably switches off her TV via her remote.* **KARA** *simultaneously does likewise. As they do this, the lights snap out on* **MURRAY** *and* **BABA***, who both exit.*

ALICE *stares at her tablet, deep in thought. In the living room,* **KARA** *rises with her cup, as* **BRAD***, in his late thirties, enters from the garden. He carries a shotgun, broken open.*

KARA Oh, there you are. You just missed it.

BRAD Missed what?

KARA The programme. On the telly. Your friend was on.

BRAD Friend?

He props the gun against the chair and, during the next, takes off his jacket.

KARA Your friend, Murray.

BRAD Oh, was he?

KARA You knew he was. With his wife. Being interviewed.

BRAD Good for him.

KARA I thought he was a friend of yours?

BRAD Twenty years ago, he was.

KARA Well, he'll be here soon, won't he? In person. I hope you'll at least look pleased to see him.

BRAD *(throwing his jacket on the settee)* He's a wally.

KARA No, he's not. He's a hero.

BRAD Once a wally, always a wally.

KARA He's got a lovely wife. Sweet little thing.

BRAD *(moving to the door)* Lucky for some, then.

KARA What's got into you this morning?

BRAD I'm going to have a shower.

KARA Brad! Don't leave that there! That gun! For God's sake! How many more times? If one of the kids touches it – Put it away, please. In the gun cupboard.

BRAD It's not loaded –

KARA You say that now – You can never be too sure, can you?

BRAD Then you put it away. *(As he leaves)* With any luck you'll blow your stupid head off...

BRAD *goes out.*

KARA Brad! Don't talk to me like that, even as a... *(Tailing off, realising she's talking to herself)* ...I hope it was a joke, anyway. I hope it was.

She sighs. She gathers up her empty cup and his discarded jacket. She hesitates. Then gingerly picks up the gun as well. She goes out after him.

In the bedroom, BABA *enters in her underslip and carrying her dress which she lays carefully on the bed. She is holding a small, well-thumbed English phrase book. She sits at the dressing table and, during the next, starts to do her make-up whilst occasionally consulting the book and mouthing phrases under her breath.*

DEREK, *forties, enters the kitchen. He is wearing his mayor's consort chain. He carries* ALICE's *more impressive mayoral one.*

DEREK Did you see it, then?

ALICE Yes, I saw it.

DEREK What were you sitting out here for? You could have seen it in there on the big screen –

ALICE Here's fine –

DEREK – in comfort.

ALICE The screen in here was quite big enough for me, thank you...

A model electric train comes out of the tunnel and stops briefly at the station. DEREK *looks at his watch.* ALICE *shuts down her tablet.*

DEREK *(with satisfaction)* Hey! Look at that! Bang on time.

As the lights turn green, the train whistles and moves on.

ALICE *(frowning)* Do they really need to run at this time of morning, Derek? Right through the kitchen?

DEREK Yes, they need to keep running, Alice. I've explained to you. The whole system's interconnected, you see. I can't shut down one branch, can I? Just the kitchen branch? It's all linked. Computer controlled, you see.

ALICE   Yes, yes, alright. It's time to leave, isn't it?

DEREK   Feeling a bit on edge, are you? Bound to be. *(Holding up her chain)* Here. I brought this up for you. Maurice brought it round.

ALICE   Thank you. Car outside, is it?

DEREK   Oh, yes, Maurice is here. Good and early, as usual. *(Helping her on with her chain)* I tested out the new branch line in the dining room, yesterday.

ALICE   *(abstracted)* Oh, good.

DEREK   It's alright, I've routed it well clear of the dining table. Besides we seldom eat in there these days, do we? Not in the dining room.

ALICE   Chance'd be a fine thing.

DEREK   *(anxiously)* You're quite sure you're up to this, love?

ALICE   I've said, I'm perfectly fine, Derek.

DEREK   I mean you don't have to go through with it necessarily –

ALICE   I have to be there. I'm the mayor –

DEREK   – people will understand, if you choose –

ALICE   Derek, for God's sake, I've stopped drinking, I've stopped smoking, if you stop me working, I really will drop dead on the spot, I promise you.

DEREK   No, I could always deputise for you. Step in, as your consort. People would understand, Alice. I'm sure they would.

ALICE   It was seventeen years ago, Derek, most of them weren't even around then, were they?

DEREK   Well, as long there isn't a – you both don't – you know –

ALICE   There isn't a what? What?

DEREK   You know – an incident? Between you and him. I mean, it would be terrible if there was an incident. I mean the press are going to be there, aren't they? If they witnessed an incident...

ALICE Derek, I promise, I shall be there in my official capacity as mayor, performing my civic duty. I shall be all smiles, I promise. I'll make a brief speech of welcome and that'll be that. Now, do come along, please. Let's get it over with...

ALICE *sweeps out, leaving* DEREK.

DEREK (*following her*) He's parked just across the road, outside Topshop... (*Having forebodings*) Oh dear...

DEREK *leaves.*

In the bedroom, BABA *at her dressing table continues to practice her colloquial English.*

BABA (*practising*) Hallo there...how simply topping to meet you...how simply topping...topping to meet you...

MURRAY *enters. He is now in his civilian jacket and trousers.*

MURRAY (*as he enters*) What did you say, Baba?

BABA Practising...see? (*Holding up her book*) Practising. How simply topping to meet you.

MURRAY Yes...very good. Excellent!

BABA Topping.

MURRAY Yes. Well done. How old is that book? *Ques anteggar bibli?*

BABA *Hiss bibli. Oh, vanitsanzu. Me patricossella sula drack. Enterniss.*

MURRAY *Su patricossella?* Your grandmother? Well, it's probably a bit out of date, love. *Ni sassa.*

BABA (*worriedly*) *Ni sassa?*

MURRAY *Ni, ni sassa.* I'll buy you something more up to date. *How drech hwecker.*

BABA *(sadly, laying the book aside)* No good – book? Bad book.

MURRAY Don't worry, darling. We'll buy you another one, won't we? Come on then! Time's getting on, now. Better get you dressed, hadn't we? *Hwanzerfrocker neeto. Vit! Vit!*

BABA *(jumping up) Hwanzerfrocker! Vit! Vit! Vit!*

She grabs up the dress and starts to struggle into it.

MURRAY No hurry! There's no hurry! More haste, less speed. Now you're getting yourself all in a tangle, aren't you? *Lantich! Baba, lantich!*

BABA *Lantich!* Sorry.

She calms and stands obediently, while he helps her to dress, as if she were a child.

MURRAY *(as he does so, reassuringly)* Now we've got some exciting days ahead of us. All this is going to be a big adventure. *Tizzernach, sooch?*

BABA *Tizzernach, sooch, sooch...*

MURRAY But we need to keep calm, darling, keep our heads. We're going to be fine, alright?

BABA Fine...

MURRAY ...everything's going to work out great...

BABA ...great...

MURRAY ...just great...

BABA ...just gre-at...

MURRAY You haven't a bloody clue what I'm talking about, have you? *(Standing back to admire her)* There you go!

BABA *(happily)* There you go!

He performs a few straightening touches as she stands obediently.

MURRAY *(indicating the door)* Ready?

BABA *(hesitating)* Wait! I need...

She searches in a drawer and takes out a screw top container of tablets.

MURRAY Baba, you don't need those now...

BABA *(struggling to get the lid off)* Sooch! Yes, yes! *(Impatiently)* Hi-yi-yi-yi!

MURRAY Here, give it me... *(He effortlessly removes the lid)*

BABA Norvous...

MURRAY Norvous? Oh, you mean nervous? *(Giving her a tablet)* Now here's <u>one</u>. Alright? You mustn't take too many at once. Dangerous. Now, do you need some wa –?

BABA *has already swallowed the tablet.*

Oh. These are not sweets, you know. They're drugs to calm you down. That's why they have these safety lids. To stop people like you from taking too many... *(He gives her back the container)*

BABA *(returning it to the drawer)* Norvous...

MURRAY Not norvous. Nervous. And you're not to be nervous, neither. Nothing to be nervous about, is there? These are friends we're going to see. Old friends. Come on then, off we go!

MURRAY *goes out.*

BABA Old friends! Yes! Off we go...

As they leave, the lights cross-fade to the living room, as BRAD *and* KARA *enter. They have changed their clothes since we last saw them and are now dressed for the formal event which is about to start in their garden.*

KARA *(as they enter)* ...I thought he was supposed to be a friend of yours? Your great childhood friend?

BRAD Once upon a time he was –

KARA You've been going on about him for years. Me and Murray, this, me and Murray, that. I'm sick to death of hearing about the bloke. Now he's actually here, you don't even want to see your old mate, apparently.

BRAD It was twenty years ago. We used to play together, that's all.

KARA Play together? What with? Wendy houses? Cowboys and Indians? Twenty years ago, you were both eighteen!

BRAD Yes, well, slightly longer than that even. Eight or nine. I can't remember.

KARA Where did you play?

BRAD Where? I don't know where. Round here usually. I had better toys. More room. Besides I think his parents were glad to get shot of him. Didn't want us kids cluttering up the hotel, did they? Getting under everyone's feet.

KARA Oh, yes, they used to run that old hotel, didn't they? Middle of town. What was it called? The Bird of Prey. Amazed your mother even allowed him in here – common publican's son, wasn't he? Not much better than I was, was he? *(Half to herself)* God, she was a snob, that woman! Thank heaven, she died before she could get her hands on our kids, that's all I can say –

BRAD *(at the window, ignoring her)* One or two starting to gather out there – the great and the good of the district. Just look at them all. Half the town council, itching to get their fingers on the cheese nibbles. Nothing like free food and drink, is there, to attract a councillor?

KARA We'll go out and join them as soon as the VIPs arrive. Just the six of us, there'll be. The lady mayor and consort, Alice and Derek, plus the guests of honour, Murray with his wife – whatsername, they did say it on the programme – something complicated and foreign, can't remember.

BRAD Is she foreign?

KARA Yes, he brought her back with him, didn't he? Back from – wherever he was – where he'd been fighting. She looks very young.

BRAD How young?

KARA Much younger than him. Than us. Early twenties? No more. Beautiful.

BRAD Bloody hell. Jammy bastard!

KARA *(amused)* Jealous? I love it when you get jealous. So used to having all the best toys, aren't you? Always have been. You can't bear it, can you, when the kid next door turns up with a shiny new fire engine?

BRAD *(muttering)* Oh, do shut up! Occasionally you're really boring, Kara...

KARA What did you both get up to then, you and Murray, when you were older? What sort of games did you play together when you were both eighteen?

BRAD I don't know. Getting drunk, driving fast cars, chasing girls...

KARA Did you ever cheat?

BRAD What?

KARA When you played your games together? Did you ever cheat in those days?

BRAD If I thought I could get away with it, I did.

KARA You used to cheat with the children. On the rare occasions you ever played with them. Monopoly. Even Ludo. You cheated at everything. Till they refused to play with you. Daisy cried for days afterwards, you know...

BRAD Great object lesson for life. Never trust your bloody parents...

KARA Going to be interesting this, isn't it? You, him and her, all in the same room? When did that last happen, I wonder?

Twenty years ago? Must have been. That's why you're in such a foul temper, isn't it? She must have been quite something, must Alice. In those days. Quite the – what d'you call it? – the femme fatale, mustn't she? Stringing you two along. Bet that took some doing.

BRAD Why don't you just shut up for a minute, eh?

KARA That the reason you've gone off your friend, is it? Still haven't forgiven him for stealing your girl? That the reason you hardly speak to her, either? Because she preferred him to you?

BRAD The reason I'm bad tempered, my love, is because I'm reminded that at the end of it all, by a cruel twist of fate I ended up with you.

The doorbell rings.

KARA *(grimly)* Thank you very much, darling. Always manage to say the right thing, don't you? That'll be them. *(As she goes)* God, the way you talk to me sometimes, Brad. If people could only hear you...

BRAD *(shouting after her)* I don't care if they do. *(To himself)* God, she drives me insane sometimes.

KARA goes out. BRAD glares after her. He moves to the garden door.

(calling to someone through the glass, affably) 'Morning, Ron. Be with you in a minute. Just waiting for the guests of honour...so far yes...it's holding off, isn't it? ...so far so good...fingers crossed, eh? See you in a bit, Ron! Try not to eat all the buns, will you? Leave one or two for us. *(He laughs)*

KARA re-enters with ALICE and DEREK.

KARA *(as they enter)* ...they could have got lost in the one way system, of course. If they're not used to it...

DEREK ...probably all changed since he was last here... Brad, mate, how you keeping...?

BRAD Alright, Derek. Good to see you.

DEREK How's everything, then?

BRAD Oh, you know, pretty fair. Thank you both for coming.

DEREK Well, we couldn't miss the hero, could we? Couldn't miss out on welcoming home the hero. I understand he was a good mate of yours?

BRAD Oh, yes. Once upon a time. A childhood chum. *(More mutedly)* Alice.

ALICE *(reserved)* Brad...

BRAD I love your necklace. I rather go for it. Don't think I've ever seen you in your full regalia, Alice, have I?

ALICE *(smiling frostily)* Goes with the job.

BRAD Yes. Congratulations. On your – on your – appointment.

ALICE Thank you.

DEREK It's just for a year. Next year, there'll be another one.

KARA Like buses, then, eh?

Slight pause as the conversation threatens to stall. The tension between **BRAD** *and* **ALICE** *is palpable.*

DEREK *(gallantly filling the breech)* Traditional of course, these chains. They go back – oh, generations... How many generations is it now, Alice? They did tell us at mayor making, do you remember?

ALICE No, I don't. I've no idea.

Slight pause.

KARA *(helping out)* Of mayors?

DEREK Pardon?

KARA Generations of mayors? Handing down their chains...?

DEREK Oh yes, goes right back to – *(To* **ALICE***)* They did say, didn't they, Alice? I forget, now. Eighteen – something...

KARA <u>Eighteen</u> something? Gracious. That is a long time ago. Fancy that. <u>Eighteen</u> something... That's interesting, isn't it, Brad?

BRAD Breathtaking.

Another silence.

DEREK Or perhaps it was only <u>nineteen</u> – something. Still, a long time ago, though.

Another silence.

KARA Yes. It's good we have these traditions, isn't it?

DEREK Well, it's part of being British, of course.

KARA Historical.

DEREK Traditional.

KARA Yes.

Pause.

DEREK How are the children then, Kara? All growing up now, I expect?

KARA Yes, they're well, thank you for asking, Derek. Simmy's – that's our eldest, Simone – she's in her last year at Greystones – hoping for university... Isn't she, Brad?

BRAD She'll be lucky.

Slight pause.

KARA And then Daisy – she's our second, she'll soon be celebrating being a teenager in a month or two... They soon grow up, don't they? And then Billy, of course, he's still the baby... I still think of him as my baby...but then, even he's – what? – this year? – what'll he be –? Eleven, come November, won't he, Brad?

Slight pause.

Yes. Eleven. Goodness. Yes. My goodness... *(Pause)* Time flies... Flies by, doesn't it? *(Pause)* Yes, it really does fly, doesn't it... Seems to fly, anyway...

Silence. KARA *finally runs out of steam.*

ALICE *(breaking the silence, impatiently)* Where the hell are these people, then? Where have they got to?

KARA They're staying out at that motor lodge on the ring road. I was saying, if they're coming from the other side of town, they may have got caught up in the new one way system. It's not easy if you're unfamiliar with it, is it?

ALICE It's not that complicated. We spent months in committee making sure it wouldn't be complicated. A child of five could find their way round it...

Slight pause.

DEREK They would have done far better if they came via the ring road. It's slightly longer that way but I find it's quicker in the long run. The other way through the town's shorter but I find it takes slightly longer in the long run. Even though it's slightly shorter. Yes...

A silence.

The doorbell rings.

ALICE At last!

KARA That'll be them.

KARA *goes out.*

DEREK *(confidentially)* I have noticed, you know. She tends to get very nervous, Kara. When she's among people. I've noticed it before. I can appreciate that, because I do as well. It's understandable, isn't it? I mean, who doesn't get nervous, now and then, eh? *(Pause)* Yes.

KARA returns with **MURRAY** *and* **BABA**, *who shyly lingers in the doorway behind the others. Suddenly, by contrast, the group explodes into life.*

KARA Here they are!

MURRAY Sorry, sorry, sorry, everyone! Are we a little bit late? You can blame that crazy one way system. Designed by lunatics, eh? *(Seeing* **BRAD**, *joyfully)* Yey – hey! Brad! There he is, the lad himself!

BRAD *(joyfully)* The hero returns! Murray, old mate!

MURRAY You bugger!

BRAD Long time, no see, you old bastard!

They go through their ritual with much embracing and slapping of palms.

The others watch with varying degrees of polite embarrassment. **ALICE** *is stone faced.*

KARA *(over the end of this)* And this is Derek, Alice's husband, Derek. You won't know him, of course, Murray.

MURRAY Hallo, Derek, pleasure to meet you.

DEREK I think we did meet briefly, way back. I did one or two jobs up at your hotel for your father. Painting and decorating. I was apprenticed to Wanston's back then.

MURRAY Oh, yes, probably. Sorry, it's been a bit of a while...

KARA And of course, you know our lady mayor, don't you?

MURRAY Yes, yes, of course. *(Slightly more restrained)* Alice.

ALICE *(coolly)* Murray.

MURRAY How goes it, then?

ALICE Still going, thank you. Just about.

MURRAY Yes. Great. That's good. Good. That's good. Good.

Slight pause as the conversation dies again.

BABA *(a small voice from behind him)* Hallo.

BRAD *(softly, seeing her for the first time, impressed)* Jesus!

MURRAY Oh! Yes, everyone, this is my wife. Sorry, darling, I'd forgotten you.

KARA *(laughing)* Isn't that a typical man? Forgetting his wife? Now, dear, we're all going to have to learn how to pronounce your name, aren't we? I heard them trying to say it earlier on the telly, but...

MURRAY Madrababacascabuna – that's just her first name. You don't even want to try with her surname. It's six yards long. Luckily everyone calls her Baba. Everybody, meet Baba. This is Baba.

KARA Hallo, Baba.

BRAD
} Baba.
DEREK

ALICE Hallo, dear.

BABA *(a rehearsed speech)* Hallo... I so pleased to be meeting with you. *(To KARA)* You have – the most – beautiful – hole. Simply peachy.

A silence.

KARA *(taken aback)* I beg your pardon?

*BRAD bellows with laughter. DEREK hides a smile.
MURRAY, too, sees the funny side. ALICE alone remains
stone-faced.*

(understanding, smiling) Oh, I see...yes... Thank you.

BABA *(confused)* Is wrong? I say wrong?

BRAD You never said a truer word, darling... I can confirm that. It's simply beautiful...none finer...

KARA ...Brad, honestly! She meant home...

BRAD ...my wife's best feature. Take it from me! Been there, done that, got the t-shirt!

KARA ...she meant home, Brad! The girl meant home!

BABA *(to* MURRAY*) Miss incaresseen?* Is wrong?

MURRAY Slightly wrong, love... I'll explain later. *Explicas. Tardee tiss explicas...*

ALICE *(briskly, clapping her hands)* If I may interrupt for a moment, please. Now that we're all gathered – at last. Can we process outside to start the ceremony. We can't keep everyone waiting any longer. Now, the procedure is as follows. The moment the guest of honour steps outside, I understand the town band will play a short fanfare. This will be followed by introductions between honoured guests and leading civic officials. There will then be a call for silence followed by more formal proceedings. I will say a few brief words of welcome – then our guest, if he so wishes, will briefly respond. I suggest it would be sensible to wrap things up in fifteen minutes at the most, as it's about to rain and none of us wishes to get soaking wet, and besides most of us have businesses to run and jobs to get on with and all are anxious to get back to them.

BRAD Alright, everyone, the mayoress has spoken, lead on...

ALICE Mayor, please, if you don't mind –

DEREK Alice prefers mayor. It's technically correct.

BRAD What's that make you, then? The mayoress?

DEREK No, I'm her consort. I'm the mayor's consort... Alright! Follow us everyone!

BRAD Oh, I see. In that case, Prince Albert, do lead on.

KARA After you, please...

ALICE *(as she leaves)* Come on, let's get it over, before it chucks it down...

ALICE *and* DEREK *go out into the garden, followed by* KARA *and* BRAD. *As the doors open, we hear the murmur of the waiting crowd.* MURRAY *holds back, waiting for* BABA *to follow.*

BABA *(tearful)* I say it wrong? Yes, I say it wrong. I shame you, Murray, I'm sorry, I'm sorry. I'm not good. For you, I'm not good.

MURRAY No, no. You're good, Baba. You're good.

BABA Yes?

MURRAY Good.

BABA Murray, why they hate you?

MURRAY What?

BABA I think they hate you. I think they do not love you, Murray. The woman with the chain...

MURRAY Alice. Oh well, she's probably...

BABA And the man. I think he is not true. Not a true man.

MURRAY What are you saying? He's my oldest friend, love. I don't know what you're talking about, I really don't –

He breaks off as KARA *reappears.*

KARA Sorry. Are you both coming out? Only everyone's waiting...

MURRAY Oh, yes of course, of course. We were just...

KARA *(as they go)* Oh, yes, it does, it looks as if it might rain in a minute...

KARA *leads them out,* MURRAY *bundling along a reluctant* BABA *before him. As they leave, the town band strikes up a fanfare. As this finishes, the chatter resumes and the full band strikes up and starts playing. As the lights cross fade to the kitchen, the sounds fade.*

ALICE *and* DEREK *enter. She seems very tense, breathing heavily as though trying to overcome a panic attack.*

DEREK ...you sure you're alright?

ALICE ...do stop fussing over me, Derek, please...!

DEREK I have to, I'm worried about you, Alice. They're starting again, aren't they? These little do's of yours? You've not had one of these for ages, have you?

ALICE *(sitting at the table)* It's nothing serious, it was just today...

DEREK Don't you think you should go straight to bed and lie down...?

ALICE ...the tension. All of us meeting up like that again...

DEREK Come on, you can't sit out here in the kitchen...

ALICE No, I'm alright, leave me now...

DEREK ...I still think you should be lying down...

ALICE *(sharply)* Derek, please. Just leave me. Flapping around me just makes it worse. Please!

A silence. He stares at her anxiously.

DEREK It really did upset you that much, didn't it? Seventeen years, Alice. It's been seventeen years, love...

ALICE Sorry. I didn't mean to snap at you.

DEREK Cup of tea?

ALICE No, thank you.

DEREK I'll make you a nice cup of tea.

ALICE I don't want a cup of tea. Please, leave me alone. Go and play with your trains. I'll be fine in a minute.

DEREK *(still reluctant to leave)* If you're quite sure?

ALICE Tell you what, you can bring me a brandy.

DEREK Oh, dear. You sure? Oh, dear...

DEREK *goes out.*

She sits there, trying to control her breathing and slow her pulse rate.

BRAD *enters from the garden.* **KARA** *follows him.*

KARA Well, I think that all went off alright, don't you? Considering. Once we were in the open air, anyway. Honestly, you two. You and her. Whatever went on there with you two? I dread to think. Honestly. And then with him. Murray. *(Pause)* It was a lovely speech.

BRAD *is silent. During the next, he opens the sideboard cupboard and takes out a bottle of single malt whisky. He pours himself a glass.*

(watching him) His speech was. Lovely, I thought. Touching. Sincere. All his secret plans for their future. I've never met a hero before, not in person. A real live hero. This place could do with a few heroes. She's nice, too, Baba. Sweet. I really took to her. Beautiful. *(Pause)* What's the matter with you, then? You know, I think maybe you're just a bit jealous, if you ask me. Of his nice shiny new fire engine. Like I used to be. Young and shiny. Just I've been left out in the rain a bit too long. One careless owner. *(Pause)* Glad she's moving here, anyway. I think, we two, we'd get on rather well. I sense we'll have a lot in common. Once we can understand each other we will, anyway.

BRAD *(laughing)* "You have a beautiful hole".

KARA Home. She meant home. A beautiful home.

BRAD There's no place like hole. Hole is where the heart is... Hole, sweet hole...

KARA Oh, shut up! She's a nice girl. She is.

BRAD I hardly spoke to her.

KARA You were staring at her enough, I noticed.

BRAD Bollocks. You think I'm after every woman, don't you?

KARA You usually are.

BRAD Think I'm after Alice then?

KARA You were. Used to be.

BRAD Ages ago, darling. Not these days. Talk about left out in the rain, she's bloody well rusted through. Off her trolley. See her today? Rushing off in the middle of Murray's speech. Poor Derek chasing after her. Both their chains clanking. Like a mayoral stampede, wasn't it?

KARA I'd love to know what really went on between those two, as well. I really would. Between her and Murray.

BRAD He left her, didn't he? He left her standing at the bloody altar. Literally standing there...

KARA Must have been more than that, surely? You get over that in time, don't you? You meet someone else. She must be over it, surely? She's happily married to Derek now, anyway. No, it's got to be something more. Something more serious. Must be...

Silence. She ponders.

You think it was that that upset her? Seeing Murray again? Him and his new wife? Maybe she was jealous? They certainly seemed very much in love, both of them. Lovely couple.

BRAD Won't last.

KARA How do you know that? How do you know?

BRAD Never does. Love's a sexual smoke screen, darling. Once it's cleared there's bugger all else there.

KARA Lovely. Thank you. I do enjoy it when you get philosophical, you know, it's so life enhancing... *(Moving to the door)* I'll leave you be then, Professor Freud. See you at dinner. It always makes you grumpy, you know, when you drink whisky.

BRAD Oh, do fuck off, there's a good girl...

KARA *goes out. In a moment,* BRAD *gets up and goes slowly out into the garden. As he does, the lights come up on the bedroom and* BABA *comes in, distressed, and sits on the bed.* MURRAY *follows her in.*

MURRAY   ...no – *nee affrontisch...vere fint hilarrous...viss intendait. Baba...*

BABA   *Nar, nar...vere affrontisch...mees humillis toos...*

MURRAY   No, you didn't. You didn't embarrass me, not at all. You heard them, didn't you? They all thought it was funny, didn't they?

BABA   I say hole? Hole is for rabbits, yes?

MURRAY   Yes, rabbits, yes.

BABA   I call her a rabbit, yes?

MURRAY   No, not really. Not at all... The word hole has various meanings, you see...

BABA   Bad meanings?

MURRAY   *(sitting beside her)* No. Yes, well. Sometimes. But then you'll find in our language that there's lots of words that can be taken different ways, you see. To mean different things... Today, my darling, you were brilliant. My little Baba was just brilliant. You understand brilliant?

BABA   *(muffled)* Brilliant...

MURRAY   Now, I said in my speech today out in that garden, that you and I we had some exciting plans to unveil – I don't know if you understood much of it – probably not – but I meant every word of it, Baba. We're here to stay, darling, us. We've come home. I ran away from here once, never again. First thing in the morning, I'm phoning Dad's solicitors to fix an appointment. Then I'll set things in motion, set our dreams in motion, darling. This is going to be your home, too, you see? From now on, I'm going to take care of you. I'll always be here for you. No need to be upset or frightened of anything or anyone. I'm here for you, darling. Don't forget, I'm a hero, aren't I? Your very own private hero, eh?

BABA *(clinging tight to him, smiling)* You – are – my – hero...

They cling together for a second.

MURRAY *(gently releasing her)* Now, I'm going to take a shower, alright? You want to share it with me? *Splizich – drizzly? Doos?*

BABA Drizzly? *Niss. In ment. Toos vende...*

MURRAY OK. Wait there. Won't be long, darling.

MURRAY goes out, starting to strip off his outer garments as he goes.

BABA sits on the bed for a moment. She gets up and goes to the dressing table. She checks that she is alone and then takes out the bottle of tablets. She struggles vainly to open it, finally gives up and returns it to the drawer. She opens her dictionary instead and thumbs through it.

In the kitchen, DEREK *returns with a modest sized glass of brandy for* ALICE, *who sits immobile.*

DEREK Sorry, we'd run out of brandy. I had to go across the precinct to the off licence. Here. There you go. *(Putting the glass gently down by her)* You sure you're alright, love?

DEREK touches her shoulder tenderly, a gesture intended to comfort her.

ALICE starts to cry quietly, rocking to and fro.

ALICE *(between her tears, wailing)* What did he want to come back for? Why did the bugger have to come back here? Why? Why?

DEREK *(alarmed by this)* Alice... Alice love...come on, now... it's alright...love... I'm here...

He continues to hold her, comforting her. In the bedroom,
BABA *is studying her book.*

BABA *(reading)* Hole...noun...aper – ture – cav – it – ee – small
place...slang word...meaning... *(Reading)* Oh, dear! Oh
goodness me! *(Swiftly closing her book)* Bad word!

As **DEREK** *continues to hold* **ALICE**, *the model train
emerges once again from its tunnel in the kitchen. It
stops briefly at the station, sounds its whistle and, once
the signal turns green, proceeds on its way, as before.*
DEREK *watches this, from over* **ALICE**'s *shoulder, checking
his watch.*

DEREK *(noting this, contentedly)* Dead on time...

The lights fade on all areas.

End of Act I Scene One

Scene Two

The lights come up on the living room.

KARA *stands by the windows, watching.*

From outside, the occasional sounds of shotgun blasts, as the three men indulge in a spot of clay pigeon shooting. Occasional shouts of triumph or disgust from one or other of them.

With each bang, **KARA** *winces slightly.*

A lull in proceedings as they reload.

After a moment, **BABA** *comes in through the other door.*

BABA *(somewhat relieved to find* **KARA***)* Ah, here!

KARA Found your way back then, did you?

BABA I was – lost. This is a big – home. Home, yes?

KARA *(smiling)* Home, yes. Very big. It's like a rabbit warren.

BABA Yes? *(Doubtfully)* Rabbit? Yes...

KARA Billy been showing you his toys, then? His toys?

BABA Oh, yes! Computers. Complicate.

KARA Don't ask me. I don't understand them, not at all. I'm hopeless. Can't even get my bloody phone to work, half the time.

BABA He is a good boy. Billy. Very kind.

KARA Yes, he is. Considerate. For that age. For a boy. Glad you got on. I knew you would.

BABA He is your – little one?

KARA Yes, Billy's our youngest. He's got two big sisters. Daisy – she's our middle one, she's just about to turn thirteen but she's not here at present, she's at boarding school – she'll be home next week for the holidays. And then there's our eldest, Simmy – that's Simone – she's seventeen. She's at home at present except she's not here, never is, she's always out, socialising. People say she's a lot like me, but I don't know – probably. We argue enough. There's times when we both –

A burst of gunfire from outside. BABA *dives for cover, covering her ears.*

BABA *(startled)* Aaaah!

KARA Oh, sorry. It's just the men. Playing with their toys. They're worse than the kids, honestly. Are you alright?

BABA Frighten. Like – home.

KARA Yes? Like at your home? Oh, yes I see. It must be. It's alright. It's quite safe. They're only shooting at clay – things – you know, pigeons.

BABA Pigeons?

KARA Yes, birds – *(Miming)* – birds – pigeons. Except they don't look like birds at all. They're clay. They look more like saucers.

BABA Saucers?

KARA Saucers. Cups and saucers. Only they're flying. Flying saucers...flying – oh, God, this bloody language, honestly – no, forget it. You're safe. Perfectly safe. Oh, yes, that reminds me, before I forget. You know you were saying you were wanting to learn English, properly...

BABA Properly English? Yes.

KARA Well, I was thinking, Simmy's old English teacher, she used to teach our Simone, Mrs Phillips, she's recently retired. She was forced to retire. They made her. She's ever such a nice woman. Said she was going mad with boredom –

BABA Mad?

KARA Being at a loose end –

BABA Loose end?

KARA She might be able to help you. She's brilliant. Anyone who can teach Simone... Mrs Phillips, Lucy, I'll put you in touch with Lucy. She's very nice. Once you get to know her. Comes over a bit fierce at first, but underneath she's –

Another burst of gunfire.

BABA *cowers again.*

Oh, God! Honestly. I don't know why he has to have it quite so near the house. We've got acres of garden, acres of it –

More gunfire. **BABA** *retreats to the doorway, as if about to take flight.*

(grabbing her by the elbow) Come on, then. I'll take you somewhere quieter. Away from the war zone – Come on!

KARA *propels* **BABA** *out of the room.*

BABA *(as they go, bewildered)* War zone? This is war zone...?

The women leave. A few more shots. Followed by a cheer.

MURRAY *enters from the garden, a shotgun broken open over his arm.* **DEREK** *follows closely behind him.*

DEREK *(as they enter, excitedly)* ...that was amazing. Brilliant shooting, Murray. If I hadn't seen it with my own eyes, I'd never have believed it –

MURRAY *(modestly)* One or two lucky shots... Reflex really...

DEREK Ah, that's what it's all about though, isn't it? Reflexes? The army did that, did it? Sharpened them up? Must have done. I expect it helps to be quick when the other side's trying to kill you, doesn't it?

MURRAY Helps a bit, yes...

DEREK I've never seen anyone beat Brad – not on that thing. Local expert, he is. Undisputed champion. Unbeatable. Till now. He was.

BRAD *comes in grimly, also carrying a broken open shotgun.*

Just saying, Brad, we got a new champion now, haven't we?

BRAD *(smiling thinly)* Yes.

He gathers up **MURRAY**'s *discarded gun and takes both weapons off into the house.*

A silence.

DEREK *(waiting till* **BRAD** *is safely out of earshot, to* **MURRAY***)* Ooops!

MURRAY *(with* **DEREK***)* Ooops! Never cares to lose, does he? I remember that from the old days. Still, understandable, isn't it? Who likes to lose, eh?

DEREK I don't mind losing. I'm used to it. I quite enjoy it, really.

MURRAY Enjoy it? What, losing?

DEREK The way I look at it someone has to lose, don't they? We can't all be winners, can we? No, it's not so much I enjoy losing, not as such. It's just I enjoy watching the other feller winning. It gives him so much pleasure winning, that sort of gives me pleasure, as well. Watching the pleasure it gives him. You follow me?

MURRAY *(mystified)* Yes. I think so.

DEREK Listen, Murray, while he's out of the room. Bit awkward this...but look, I hope you're not planning on sticking around here for too long, are you?

MURRAY Why?

DEREK *(embarrassed)* Well, you'll be aware you've created a bit of an atmosphere, both of you. You and Baba. You're probably aware.

MURRAY With Alice?

DEREK Well, mostly with Alice, yes. Since she heard you were coming back, she's been in a bit of a bad way...it seems it's affected her... I mean, all the stuff that happened between you two was before my time, of course, before I came properly on the scene... But I care about her a lot, Alice. And for her sake...in my humble opinion...the sooner you leave here, the better.

MURRAY No, I'm staying, Derek.

DEREK What?

MURRAY This is my home. I intend to stay here. Both of us are staying.

DEREK *(nonplussed)* Oh. Right. Fair enough.

BRAD *returns. He seems to have recovered.*

BRAD Nice shooting, old boy.

MURRAY Just saying, probably a bit of luck involved. Beginner's luck, you know.

DEREK What? You mean, you've never done it before? Clay pigeon shooting?

MURRAY First time. If it's any consolation.

BRAD Well, no, it isn't really. Not at all. Being beaten by an expert is one thing but being beaten by some bugger who didn't even have an effing bloody clue what he was doing is quite another. *(He laughs)*

DEREK Two out of two now, isn't it? Yesterday the snooker. Then today the shooting. That was brilliant yesterday, Murray mate. I tell you, I could have been watching, whatsisname, you know the one on telly. The way you cleared that table – incredible – one – two – three...

BRAD *(smiling)* Yes, I'd prefer you didn't go on about that either, Derek, if you don't mind.

DEREK Oh, sorry. Sorry. *(Pause)* ...Red...colour...red...colour... *(He clicks his tongue, miming a few snooker shots)* Brilliant!

MURRAY One or two lucky breaks...

BRAD Don't tell me you've never played that before, either.

MURRAY Not that often. Not since I've been abroad –

DEREK That's even more amazing. Seventeen years...

Pause.

MURRAY Look, I must find Baba. We need to get off. I've got an appointment with our solicitor. They said he'd be back this afternoon. I fixed a meeting.

BRAD Why are you seeing him? If you don't mind my asking?

MURRAY Well, it's...it's still all in the air at present. Nothing's settled yet. No, what's the harm? – I can tell you two. The fact is I've – we've been thinking about – making plans for our old family hotel, you know –

DEREK What, The Bird of Prey?

MURRAY Yes, I've been dreaming about doing something with it for the past few months. Even while I was still overseas. Ever since I knew I was coming home, been dreaming up plans. First thing I did, soon as we arrived here, I went to see my dad in the nursing home – I wanted to discuss it with him first, you know – about the hotel – because technically, of course, he still owns it. Only he had to give up the running of it because of his health. I've passed it a couple of times since we've been back. It's just sitting there, isn't it, going to waste. Crying shame. Tragic, really. Hardly bear to look at it –

DEREK Listen, I understood that The Bird of Prey was... *(He tails off)*

MURRAY What?

DEREK *(with a glance at* **BRAD***)* Oh, nothing... Probably rumours. Nothing.

MURRAY What rumours? Rumours I should know about?

DEREK No, I was just going to say, I heard the building's in a shocking state. These days, it's an eyesore. Slap in the middle of the town centre, too. We live opposite it. We have to look at it every day. Slowly rotting away.

MURRAY It used to be my home. I grew up there. You remember it, Brad, The Bird of Prey? Back in the old days? We had some times up there, didn't we? Between us?

BRAD *and* MURRAY *exchange looks.*

A pause.

DEREK *(intrigued)* Hallo, hallo. What happened, then? Between you two?

MURRAY *(rising, suddenly)* I must find Baba. *(He moves to the door)* I'll look in again before we go.

MURRAY *goes out.*

DEREK *(cheerfully)* Alright then, don't tell me. See if I care.

BRAD Nothing you'd want to hear about, Derek. You don't need to know too much about our insalubrious past...

DEREK Listen, I didn't like to say this, not in front of him, but Alice was telling me that The Bird of Prey is scheduled for demolition, you know.

BRAD Yes, I'd heard that.

DEREK His family doesn't even own it. After his mother died, once his dad started hitting the bottle, you know, he'd re-mortgaged it that many times that eventually the bank stepped in, of course. And finally it passed to the council. According to Alice – they've applied for draft planning permission to demolish it and they plan to replace it with upmarket retail units and town centre luxury apartments. I mean, that's the plan. Early stages, of course, pending an appeal. Probably shouldn't be telling you this... It's grade two listed but it's in such a shocking state they don't anticipate a problem. The last thing this town needs is another bloody pub in the centre. I mean, I'm amazed Murray's dad didn't say anything to him. Maybe the old boy's out of it. Or maybe he didn't deliberately. Still hasn't forgiven Murray for running out on his wedding day. That's what finished his mother, apparently, Alice says. Apparently, she never properly recovered. Her health went right down hill from that day on. Shock, you know. That's what I heard from Alice, anyway.

Slight pause. **BRAD** *reflects.*

BRAD Had my first drink in that place, you know. The Bird of Prey. My first alcoholic drink. I was thirteen years old. Down in the cellar.

DEREK What was the drink? Can you remember that?

BRAD Vodka and vintage cider...

DEREK Never tried that. Good, was it?

BRAD I was sick for days. Put me off vintage cider for life. You tend to remember those things. Your first proper drink. Your first cigarette. Your first proper woman.

DEREK Who was your first proper woman, then?

BRAD Room nine. Where I first had sex with a woman. You know, the full works. Touching all the bases. Also at The Bird of Prey. Room nine. Smoked my first cigarette in there, too. Straight afterwards. She introduced me into some wicked ways, did that one.

DEREK Ah. Lot happened in that place from the sound of it. Who was she, then? This wicked woman?

BRAD Can't remember at all. They all blur into one, old boy, after a time.

DEREK Funny you recalling the room number, your cigarette and the drink but you can't remember her name, though, isn't it?

BRAD Yes. Odd thing, the memory...

KARA *appears in the doorway. Behind her are* MURRAY *and* BABA.

KARA They're just off.

BRAD *(not moving)* Jolly good. Cheerio.

DEREK *(rising half-heartedly)* Yes, well...

MURRAY See you soon, then. Re-match next week maybe, Brad?

BRAD It's a date. I owe you one, boy.

MURRAY Bye!

MURRAY *goes off with* KARA.

BABA *lingers behind briefly.*

BABA *(flashing them a dazzling smile)* Bye-bye!

The two men watch her leave, focussing on her retreating backside.

They growl.

BRAD Would you get a load of that? Wouldn't mind a slice of that, eh? Tasty or what?

DEREK T-a-a-a-sty! *(Slight pause)* Ah, well, what do they say? One can but dream, eh?

BRAD How do you mean?

DEREK She's his wife, isn't she?

BRAD How long's that going to last, do you think?

DEREK Well. Who can tell? They seem very much in love.

BRAD She's got the hots for him, that's why. A semi-literate kid from some third-world backwater, hardly speaks English. Gets her into bed with him and he fucks her tiny brains out. She doesn't know what's hit her. Once she comes down to earth, realises what an idiot she's shacked up with...

DEREK *(dubiously)* You think so?

BRAD I've known dozens of girls like that. They're like cats, most of them. Saucer of milk's big enough, they're anyone's. Rubbing up against your legs... Miaou!

DEREK Do you think she'd – not that I would, mind – but do you think she'd – with me then, do you?

BRAD Well, when I say 'anyone' I think even she'd draw the line somewhere, Derek... Not quite a big enough saucer, old chap.

DEREK No. I'm not serious. One can but dream. And I do have my Alice, of course.

BRAD Of course.

DEREK And you have Kara, of course.

BRAD She's no problem. Does as she's damn well told, does Kara.

DEREK Well...

BRAD Tell you what – You a betting man? – 'course you are – I bet you a thousand quid I could –

DEREK *(alarmed)* A <u>thousand</u>?

BRAD Five hundred then – five hundred quid – I can have her – that little girl – whatsername –

DEREK Baba...

BRAD Baba – what sort of name is that, for Christ's sake? – I can take her off Murray inside a month – no, I can do better than that – inside a fortnight. Alright? Done? Deal?

DEREK You don't really mean that, do you?

BRAD I certainly do. *(Extending a hand)* Done, then? Is it a deal? Come on!

DEREK *(touching* **BRAD**'s *hand, weakly)* Done.

KARA *returns.*

KARA You know, she's lovely, that girl, I've really taken to her – what you both doing? – she's promised to baby-sit, Brad, that's convenient, isn't it?

BRAD *(as he goes)* Oh, that's great news, darling. Ideal. Couldn't have worked out better for all of us.

BRAD *goes out.*

KARA *(following him out, puzzled)* What's he on about now? What are you on about now...?

DEREK *(concerned, to himself)* God, I think he actually means it. He does, he means it!

As he follows them out, the lights cross fade to the kitchen as **ALICE** *enters having just admitted* **MURRAY**. *She carries her tablet which is up and running.*

ALICE *(entering, coolly)* ...you don't mind being in the kitchen, do you?

MURRAY *(as he follows her)* ...sorry, Alice, I hope I'm not interrupting anything important, am I?

ALICE No, it's just routine. I can do a lot of work from home, these days, thanks to this thing...

MURRAY What is it you do exactly?

ALICE Property. Buy and sell it mainly. Develop it. Derek's in the building trade. Now, what can I do for you, Murray? Do sit down. I won't offer you a cup of tea, if you don't mind. I've just had one.

MURRAY *(slightly disconcerted by her abruptness)* No, that's OK... I didn't – I didn't really want... Really. *(Pause)* I like your railway out there.

ALICE Sorry?

MURRAY Your model railway. Out there in the hall. Oh, and it's even in here, I see.

ALICE Yes, it's everywhere. We have trains everywhere.

MURRAY Ah. Comprehensive layout, then? You're enthusiasts, I take it?

ALICE They even run through the linen cupboard. It's Derek's hobby, rather than mine –

MURRAY Oh. Do you mind me asking, does it run through your bedroom as well?

ALICE *(rather abruptly)* What is it you wanted to talk to me about, Murray?

MURRAY *(gathering his thoughts)* Ah. Yes... Well, I've just been in with Barry. Barry Wilkinson...

ALICE Oh, yes, the solicitor. I know Barry very well...

MURRAY ...as you may know, he mainly acted for my parents, when they were both – active, you know...

ALICE Yes, I knew that.

MURRAY And I've just spent over an hour with him – and he's put me in the picture regarding our hotel. You see, I – we had planned to reopen it. Baba and me. Give it a complete makeover, upgrade it. The public rooms, to start with. And one or two of the bedrooms. They're in a shocking state and as for the kitchens...

ALICE Yes, I gathered that was your intention. Cost a small fortune, you know.

MURRAY Well, I've quite a bit saved. And I was hoping to obtain a loan for the remainder...just temporarily, you know. And when I talked it over with my dad a few days ago, he seemed all for the idea.

ALICE *(dryly)* Did he, now?

MURRAY But I understand from Barry, just now, that there's one or two stumbling blocks...

ALICE One or two. Like your father doesn't even own it. Not any more.

MURRAY So it appears.

ALICE We do. The council does.

MURRAY Yes, so I understand now. And Barry said you were possibly the person to talk to. Seeing as you're the chairman of the relevant committee –

ALICE The chair, yes.

MURRAY Sorry, the chair –

ALICE Although, since my appointment as mayor, I no longer serve as chair on that particular committee, of course –

MURRAY Ah, perhaps I'm speaking to the wrong person, then –

ALICE – although as mayor, I do chair all regular meetings of full council before which this business will undoubtedly come in due course, so in effect you are talking to the right person.

MURRAY *(a trifle confused)* Ah, yes. Well, so I thought I'd have a word with the chair. I mean, I wouldn't normally – given our previous personal history, Alice – but I wondered if you'd be prepared to bury the – I mean, even supposing there is one to bury – I don't know if there even is one now, but I sense there might be one still –

ALICE Oh, yes. It's still there. Whilst you've been gallivanting round the world, Murray, the rest of us have had to stay put. There's still a hatchet. Very much so.

MURRAY *(laughing)* Yes, well, hopefully the burial service follows shortly, eh? But in the meantime – why I'm here, I was wondering if, in your capacity as – chair, you might be able to suggest a way forward, Alice? I mean, it's – let's face it, this town could do with a decent first class hotel, couldn't it? Slap in the town centre? Crying out for one, isn't it? Don't you agree?

ALICE Well, I can make one suggestion. You could start by changing the name. Rather than Bird of Prey you could rename it Pie in the Sky.

MURRAY *(digesting this)* I see. That's your feeling on the matter, is it?

ALICE It's being torn down, Murray. It's going to be demolished.

MURRAY I understand it's listed, though...

ALICE Yes, we are appealing that. Considering the current state of the building, it's in the interests of public safety that it comes down. We've a strong case for demolition. The last thing we need in the middle of this place is another glorified pub. What we need is to restore the town's heart by providing high quality town centre accommodation and a few more up-market retail units –

MURRAY But surely, can't there be a bit of everything?

ALICE Murray, I live here. I look out of that window on to that precinct every single night – Sunday to Thursday it's like a ghost town out there. Fridays and Saturdays, it's worse than Gomorrah. Kids fighting, throwing up, can of alcohol in one hand, mobile phone in the other. Like a swarm of vomiting fireflies. Disgusting.

MURRAY Not like in our day, then?

ALICE Nothing like in our day. I'm sorry, Murray. The sooner that place goes, the better for all of us.

MURRAY (*moving to the window*) If you feel that way, I'm surprised you've chosen to live here bang opposite. Staring straight at it, aren't you?

ALICE Someone has to live here. We're the only people keeping the town alive. Keeping its heart beating. If we leave, it'll stop for ever. May as well tear the rest of it down, then.

MURRAY Lot of memories wrapped up in that place, The Bird of Prey, aren't there? For both of us. Remember the room?

ALICE (*smiling grimly*) Room nine.

MURRAY Room nine. Well remembered. It was the only one with a decent sized double bed, wasn't it? Used to call it the bridal suite.

ALICE (*smiling, thinly*) Sick joke in the circumstances...

MURRAY You've changed quite a bit, Alice, since those days...

ALICE I hope to God I have...

MURRAY When I first saw you, I hardly recognised you. You were always a tough woman. Now you're hard. Listen, I'm not giving up, you know. There's a lot of my life tied up in that place.

ALICE There's a lot of mine there, too, Murray, in case you'd forgotten.

Pause. They seem to have reached an impasse.

Listen, you want a bit of advice? Leave now. Today. Just go far away, far as you can, you and your little bride. Start a new life in John o' Groats or somewhere. Just go!

MURRAY Goodbye, Alice. Thanks for the advice. Won't keep you any longer. I'll leave you to get on with your – business.

ALICE Thank you.

MURRAY *(in the doorway)* By the way, that proposed development across the road. You wouldn't happen to have a private interest in the building of that by any chance, would you?

ALICE Nothing you could prove...

As MURRAY *goes out, the model train passes again, giving its familiar cheery whistle.* ALICE *sits for a second glaring at her screen. Then, with a growl of irritability, she closes the machine and exits with it under her arm. As she does so, the lights cross fade back to the living room.* KARA *enters with* BABA.

KARA ...now, Daisy's upstairs in her room doing her revision. And Billy's meant to be doing his homework – only I bet he'll be playing with his blessed PlayStation...

BABA Oh, yes they are very – addictive, aren't they?

KARA Oh, That's a good word. Addictive. You've been doing your homework too, I see, haven't you? That'll be Lucy Phillips, then?

BABA Yes, Lucy. She is excellent. Very big help for me. She is – she is –

KARA *(helping her out)* Strict? Lucy can be very strict? Strict, yes? Stern?

BABA *(finding the word)* ...Punctilious...

KARA Good gracious!

BABA It's wrong? Not a right word?

KARA No, quite right. Yes, good word. Probably. I'm not quite sure precisely what it means, actually... It's not a word I tend to use that much.

BABA Not a good word? You don't use?

KARA Not every day...not in this house... Our words usually have slightly fewer letters. Now, as I was saying, we shouldn't either of us be that late. I'm just out to dinner with these friends – we're trying out that new restaurant in the Square. Heard good reports, so we'll see. And Brad's at some meeting or other. He was supposed to eat with us as well, till he remembered he had this meeting. He shouldn't be too late either. Don't worry, I'll be back in good time, you won't be on your own for long.

BABA And is Simmy...?

KARA No, Simmy's not here. She's staying over with a friend. As usual. A girl friend. I hope it's a girlfriend, anyway. You never know these days. No, she's a sensible girl, is Simmy. Responsible. I don't need to worry about her. Oh, look at the time. Do you want to come upstairs now? Say a quick hallo? Then I'll show you where we keep everything. Tea, coffee, whisky, gin, whatever you fancy...

BABA No, no. No gin, no...

KARA Well, whatever. Feel free to help yourself...

As they leave the sitting room, the lights cross fade back to the kitchen as DEREK *and* ALICE *enter.*

DEREK ...he came here, you say?

ALICE ...just walked in...

DEREK What did he want?

ALICE What do you think? He'd found out about his precious
hotel – that it didn't even belong to him... I think he was
going to try and talk me round but I soon stopped that –

DEREK I don't believe this. He tried to talk you round? Like
you owed him a favour? I can't believe he'd do that. I can't
believe anyone would do that.

ALICE Forget about it, Derek, he's not worth it –

DEREK No, I'm getting angry, Alice. I'm getting angry for you.
You don't often see me angry, do you, but I'm getting angry
now...

ALICE ...forget it, Derek...

DEREK ...really angry... I'm livid... I'm beside myself... I'm
hopping mad, Alice...no, really...how dare he? How bloody
dare he?

ALICE Derek! Calm down. Look at me. Do you see me angry?
I'm not angry, darling. I'm the one who should be angry...

DEREK Well, someone's got to be angry for you, Alice. He leaves
you standing at the altar... His fiancée of six months...
Carrying his child...

ALICE Don't dig all that up again, for God's sake...

DEREK ...and then to cap it all he creeps back three days later,
doesn't he, and burns your bloody cottage down...?

ALICE ...we don't know that for sure...

DEREK ...the cottage his parents had bought out of their life
savings...

ALICE It wasn't their life savings, Derek. They never bought
that cottage for us. It wasn't them who bought it. Think they
could have afforded it, those two? Running a hotel mortgaged
to the hilt, both of them drinking the profits away?

DEREK Then who bought them the cottage, then? The one he burnt down?

ALICE We don't even know it was Murray burnt it down. It was never proved he started the fire... Forget all about that.

DEREK Well, who was it did buy the cottage for you? Who? Alice? I want to know. Tell me.

The train arrives at the station and goes through its routine.

ALICE Derek, if we have to discuss this, would it be possible, please, to switch off these bloody trains? Just for a moment, please. I'm sorry, but –

DEREK I can't do that, you know that. Shut it all down. It'll take me days to reset the programme – No, tell me, I want to know, Alice. Who bought the cottage for you, then?

ALICE *(a slight pause)* Brad's parents. They bought it. Sir David Seymore-Watkin MP and Lady Muckface. They didn't even have to buy it. It was part of their estate, wasn't it?

DEREK Why give it to you and Murray? I don't understand.

ALICE *(shrugging, evasively)* Who knows? Maybe Brad had a word with them. Persuaded them. Maybe wanted to help out his mate, I don't know. A wedding present, perhaps?

DEREK Hell of a wedding present. A whole cottage.

ALICE For a wedding that never was, yes. Let's not talk about it any more, Derek, if you don't mind... I'm feeling a bit...

DEREK *(concerned)* No, of course, love. Are you alright?

ALICE Yes. A little dizzy, that's all...

DEREK It's his fault, bursting in here like that, without warning... I had a word with him too, you know... When I was round at Brad's. Hey, you should have seen him, Alice. Murray. You should have seen that lad shoot. Trounced Brad good and proper. I think, underneath, Brad was secretly hopping mad. You know how Brad hates to lose. At anything. Hates it. I remember the one occasion I beat him at table tennis, he wouldn't talk to me for days...

ALICE Oh, they're at it again, are they? Competing? Betting against each other? Guess who's best? *(Rising)* I'm just going to lie down for a minute, alright?

DEREK *(rising)* Right. Betting? What sort of betting? What did they used to bet on, then?

ALICE Oh, you name it. Anything you can do, I can do better. Men like that, once they get going. Everything. Sport. Physical dares. Women...

ALICE goes out.

DEREK Women...? *(Digesting this for a second, appalled)* Oh, God! What have I done? What the hell have I started?

DEREK hurries from the room after ALICE. As he goes, the lights cross fade to the living room as BABA enters.

BABA *(calling back to someone)* Alright, Daisy. OK. I'll be down here, OK? *(Sitting on the sofa, to herself)* Yes. This is a nice house. Very nice house. Big house. Comfy house.

She rummages in her bag and produces an exercise book and a small English dictionary. She opens her book to reveal neatly hand written columns of words. Her own 'homework' presumably, set by the punctilious Lucy Phillips.

(reading slowly) ...Men – a – cing...menacing. Om – min – ous...ominous. Pre – dat – tory ... predatory. Good. Sin – is – ter...sinister...

A rapping on the garden door. BABA reacts nervously. Further rapping. She moves cautiously to investigate.

(seeing who it is) Ah! Wait...

She goes and unlocks the door and admits BRAD.

BRAD Sorry if I frightened you. Forgot my wretched front door keys. I'd have rung the bell only I didn't want to wake the kids...

BABA No, they are still awake. At least Daisy. I think Billy maybe... You are home early?

BRAD Idiotic, me. Went to the meeting – turned out I had the wrong week. *(He laughs)*

BABA *(laughing, too)* Oh, silly...

BRAD *(laughing)* One of these days I'll forget my head, won't I...?

BABA *(laughing)* Oh, yes. Forget your head. Very good.

BRAD Well, I see you've made yourself nice and cosy, anyway.

BABA Yes. Nice and cosy. Good warm house...

BRAD What's all that you've been up to, then?

BABA Ah, sorry no – sorry... *(She makes to clear things away)* It is just my English work...

BRAD No, great. Leave it. That's fine. I'm just going to pour myself a drink, if you don't mind. You fancy one? Scotch?

BRAD moves to the sideboard and produces the bottle of single malt and a couple of glasses.

BABA Oh, no, no, thank you...

BRAD Oh, come on, join me. Just the one. No harm in one, surely? This is a quite exceptional single malt. Not widely known but, in my opinion, one of the very best. You ever tried single malt?

BABA No, not single malt...no...

BRAD *(handing her a glass)* Here, you try that. You'll find that is special. Drop of good Scotch, just the thing to help you with your English, eh? Here's looking at you, darling.

BRAD raises his glass and takes a swill.

BABA *takes a tentative sip.*

BABA *(half choking)* Oh, goodness...*seer crassa salva...*

BRAD You OK?

BABA It is...for cleaning...yes?

BRAD Cleaning? I don't think the distillers would love you for that... Now, take small sips...sip it...in a minute or two, you'll start to feel the benefit...

BABA *(hoarsely)* ...my throat, it is...broken...

BRAD Tell you what, while we're here, I'll give you a hand with your English, shall I? *(He picks up her dictionary)* Teach you a few fresh words...

BABA Oh, no, no... Mrs Phillips...she... Lucy is already teaching...

BRAD What, old Lucy Phillips? Bet she'll never teach you words like these, darling... Now take your drink, sit down over here... come on, sit! Sit!

BABA *sits, meekly holding her glass.*

That's better. Now, take another sip. You want to be English, don't you? Well if you want to be English, darling, you're going to have to learn to drink Scotch. Forget all that foreign muck. Schnapps and Schlitz...

BABA I don't drink these things, I drink nothing – I –

BRAD *gestures sternly for her to drink. She meekly obeys, sipping again.*

(reacting) It is a terrible drink...

BRAD Acquired taste. *(Rifling through the pages)* Now then, let's find a nice juicy word for you...ah, here's a good one! Right, say after me...tan – ta – li – sing...say that, then...

BABA Tanta –

BRAD Tanta – lising...

BABA Tanta – lising...

BRAD You know what that means?

BABA No...

BRAD It means – pro – voc – ative...

BABA Pro – voc – ative... Is a good word...?

BRAD Very good word. Provocative. Very good word. Well done.

BABA Thank you.

She absent-mindedly takes another sip of her drink. She immediately regrets it.

(reacting) Chowsss! Ah!

BRAD Here's another one... Titi – llating...

BABA Titi – llating...is a pretty word...

BRAD Yes, it is. You know what it means –? That pretty word?

BABA No.

BRAD *(moving to sit beside her)* It means far more than pretty – it means – ir – res – is – tible...something you can't resist... something you can barely keep your hands off... Here's another one. Suc – cu – lent...say that...

BABA ...suc – cu – lent...

BRAD ...se – duc – tive...

BABA ...se – duc – tive...

BRAD ...sen – su – ous...

BABA *(seemingly hypnotised)* ...sen – su – ous...

BRAD ...sex   ual...

BABA ...sex – *(Her alarm bells starting to ring)* Oh, no, no, no, no, no... *(She draws away from him)* Sex, no! Bad word. Bad!

BRAD Bad? Sex? Nothing wrong with sex, darling. It can be bad. It can be magical. In the right hands. Depends whose hands you're in, who you do it with...

BABA I do it with Murray. Sex. Only with Murray. I vow.

BRAD And Murray? Does he just do it with you? Sex? Just with you?

BABA Yes.

BRAD You sure?

BABA He vowed also.

BRAD *sighs a deep sigh of sadness. He shakes his head.*

What? Why you make these noises? Why?

BRAD Let me tell you something about Murray, darling. He's my oldest and dearest friend and I love him almost as much as you love him, if that's possible...but he and I, we go back a long way. Over twenty years, before you were born, probably...and we grew up together, sharing our toys, hobbies...you following this, are you...?

BABA Yes, I'm following this, yes –

BRAD And then, later on, as we became adult, you know, well, naturally we both became interested in girls. Early on, as you do, just for a bit of fun, you know. On both sides. For them and us. I'd go out with a girl one night and she'd go off with Murray the next. We shared, you know. Just as we'd always shared. And then one day – it had to happen, of course, sooner or later. I fell in love. I fell in love with the most beautiful woman I'd ever met in my life. She was a student down from London, doing a holiday job in the local hotel, as a chamber maid. We were so much in love – and we both knew – even though we were seventeen, eighteen years old – that this was it. It was a perfect summer together. And at the end of it we became unofficially engaged. But the big problem was Murray. He refused to accept it. He became very jealous. Crazy with jealousy. This girl had stolen away his friend, you see. How dare she? Till then he and I were inseparable. And now here I was sneaking away at all hours to be with her. He just couldn't accept it...he couldn't...he... he... *(He stops suddenly as if overcome by his narrative)*

BABA *(spellbound by this)* Please...tell me...what did Murray do...?

BRAD This mustn't go any further than here, please. If anyone knew I'd told you this – especially Murray –

BABA Tell me, what did Murray do? This woman, she was Alice, yes...?

BRAD Yes...

BABA ...I know something happened which made Murray leave here with a bad feeling. What did he do? Please tell me.

BRAD He took Alice away from me...

BABA But she was with you. She was engaged to you?

BRAD Yes.

BABA But she leave you...? To go with Murray?

BRAD Yes...

BABA Even though she did not love him?

BRAD I don't believe she did...

BABA But she agree to marry him?

BRAD Yes.

BABA Why?

BRAD Because he'd made her pregnant, that's why.

BABA *(her hand to her mouth)* Oh, madraymiscous!

BRAD She was expecting his child. Until he runs away and leaves her at the last minute – *(He appears to be on the verge of tears)*

BABA *(in shock)* Murray? This is true? It's true?

BRAD I'm sorry. I didn't mean to tell you that bit. Sorry.

> **BRAD** *holds out his arms to her. She responds, clinging to him. She starts to cry.* **BRAD** *strokes her reassuringly.*

(gently) It's alright...It's alright. I'm here, darling. I'm here for you...

He gently releases her and allows her to ease back onto the sofa. He strokes her hair from her face and kisses her gently.

(softly and coaxingly) It's alright...it's alright...darling... I'm here, now...it's alright...

BRAD *starts gently to un-button her blouse.*

(as he does so) Shh! Shh, now... Forget about him, eh?

He slips his hand inside her blouse.

You forget Murray...forget that bastard...there, that's better...

BABA *(reacting, violently, loudly)* No, no, NO! *(She jumps to her feet)*

BRAD *(irritated, so near and yet so far)* Oh, come on...

BABA *(vehemently)* You're bad! You're bad! Bad person!

She re-buttons her blouse and gathers up her things. She moves to the door.

BRAD Where are you going?

BABA *(yelling and pointing at him)* MEN – A – CING! OM – IN – OUS! ...PRE – DA – TORY!

BRAD What the hell you talking about?

BABA *(screaming)* SIN – IS – TER! SIN – IS – TER! SIN – IS – TER!

She pauses for breath, panting. **BRAD** *stands, undecided whether to pursue or give up. From upstairs a girl's voice is heard calling.*

DAISY *(off, calling)* Baba! Baba! Anything wrong? Baba!

BRAD *(reacting to this, softly)* Shit!

He moves quickly to the door. **BABA** *eludes his advance and makes a dash past him and rushes out of the garden door, grabbing up her belongings as she goes.*

(as this happens, calling) It's alright, Daisy, darling! I'm home now! Dad's here!

DAISY *(offstage, calling)* Dad? I heard shouting. Is Baba alright?

BRAD It's alright, now, darling! Go back to bed! Try and get some sleep! Everything's fine, now.

BRAD *listens at the door and then hurries to the garden door.*

(calling softly) Baba! Baba...? Baba!

Receiving no reply, he turns back into the room.

Shit! Shit! Shit! Stupid bitch!

After a second he goes off.

As he does so, the lights cross fade to the bedroom. **BABA** *enters hurriedly, still slightly distressed.* **MURRAY** *follows her, anxiously.*

MURRAY *(as they enter)* ...you mean you walked home?

BABA Yes.

MURRAY Right round the ring road? On your own? I was going to collect you later, darling! You didn't walk all that way, did you?

BABA No, I did not walk. I was running. Running!

MURRAY *(attempting to take hold of her, concernedly)* Baba, what's happened, darling? What's wrong?

BABA *(shrugging him away)* There is nothing wrong...nothing! Please!

MURRAY *(gently)* Baba, you have to tell me, what's happened to you? You need to tell me, love.

BABA *(stiffly)* I need to tell you nothing. I do not wish to account for my actions, like I am a child. I am a grown woman.

MURRAY *(crouching beside her, gently)* Baba... Baba...come on now, Baba...

BABA *(loudly and angrily)* My name is not Baba! That is not my name! My name is Madrababacascabuna!

 MURRAY *is startled by her uncharacteristic vehemence. He rises.*

MURRAY *(a little shaken)* I'll just go and have a shower. We can talk about it later.

BABA *(quietly)* Yes, we can. *(Half to herself)* We can talk about it later, yes.

 MURRAY *gives her a nervous glance and goes off.* BABA *sits for a moment and takes several deep breaths to calm herself. She rises and goes to her dressing table. She takes her notebook and dictionary, once again from her bag. Music starts under the next.*

 (resuming her studies) ...En – deavour...endeavour. En – counter... encounter. Con – flict...conflict. Bat – tle...battle. Hostil – it – ies...hostilities. Act – ion...action. Good. *(Firmly)* Yes. Action!

 The lights fade on her to: –.

 A blackout.

End of Act 1 Scene Two

ACT II

Scene One

The kitchen. ALICE *enters with* BABA. *The latter is dressed in her street campaigning attire with a badge: Save The Bird of Prey.*

ALICE *(as they enter)* ...what are you doing out there, anyway, all of you?

BABA We are saving the hotel, The Bird of Prey. It is an endangered species. That is our catchword. We have, besides this, an on-line website. And for sale from the trellis table down there, flags, posters and for the children, small stuffed birds.

ALICE *(mildly amused)* Well, I have to hand it to you, you've got a hell of a nerve, haven't you? Setting it up under my very window, all your paraphernalia with your trestle tables...

BABA *(fiercely to herself)* trestle...trestle...not trellis...trestle table...

ALICE Your English is coming on, anyway.

BABA Yes, it is. Lucy says I am an exemplary student and I'm making spectacular progress...

ALICE *(dryly)* Well, don't use too many long words round here will you, dear, or half the people still won't understand you. So tell me, what are you hoping to achieve by all this? What are you hoping to accomplish?

BABA *(the official line)* We are hoping to achieve by all this the saving of a beautiful grade two listed historical hotel. To re-open it in all its foremost glory as an old-style coaching house but also as a fully modernised gastro pub. Five star.

ALICE Best of luck.

BABA Thank you.

ALICE It's a dump, love. It's an eyesore. Have you been inside? Have you had a look inside?

BABA No, we cannot. Unfortunately they will not allow.

ALICE It's disgusting. The carpets are rotting, half the ceilings are caving in, the walls are dripping – as for the roof – there's enough birds of prey roosting up there to start a pigeon farm.

BABA Yes, yes, of course, it needs work, it needs investing... but we are planning...

ALICE It needs pulling down, dear! The sooner the better. The whole thing'd be a fire hazard, if it wasn't so damp. Listen, I don't know why you've come to see me, I really don't. I presume your husband put you up to this, hoping you'll talk me round –

BABA No, this is me. This is not Murray. Not at all is it Murray, it is me...

ALICE Because I'm telling you what I told him a week ago. One way or another, that place is going to be demolished. It's council owned and it's solely up to the council to determine its future –

BABA No, it is not solely up to you, it is a listed building –

ALICE Which we are appealing to have de-listed –

BABA And which we are opposing against!

A pause.

It seems that in determination the two are closely matched.

So. We shall see, yes? What transpires?

ALICE We certainly will. *(Staring at* **BABA***)* You know, I rather underestimated you, when I first met you. Quite a little powerhouse, aren't you, in your own way? Not quite so green as you're cabbage looking. Murray's certainly landed on his feet, come out smelling of roses, hasn't he?

BABA I have no idea what you are speaking about. Green cabbages and feet smelling of roses? I'm sorry? I love Murray. This is true.

ALICE I'm sure you do. He's quite easy to love, is Murray.

BABA Oh, yes.

ALICE He's someone who's there for you. Know what I'm saying?

BABA I think so. He's all there.

ALICE Never have to waste your life trying to second guess him, do you? You never have to think, like you do with some men, what's the bugger up to now? Now what's he thinking? Does he really mean that, or does he mean just the opposite? All that might be very attractive to start with but it soon gets tiring. Enigmatic men! Give me an honest, simple one, every time.

BABA Oh, yes, Murray is honest. He has faults. But they are correctable.

ALICE If you're lucky, they are.

BABA You also loved Murray, I think?

ALICE I did once. Don't worry, I'm well over him now. I've got Derek. Murray mark two. Even more honest and reliable. Maybe not quite so glamorous but at least he's still here and didn't bugger off halfway through.

BABA He left you in the church? With his baby?

ALICE *(slightly sharply)* Who told you that?

BABA *(guardedly)* I heard from – someone...

ALICE Well, they told you wrong, love. Whoever it was, misinformed you. I was pregnant but it wasn't Murray's child.

BABA But he was engaged to you. Murray was your fiancé.

ALICE These things happen. We have this saying, 'having a misspent youth'. Me? By the time I was twenty, I'd misspent so much I was bankrupt...

BABA *Oh, shheeewan!* Of course! It was with Brad, your baby?

ALICE Right.

BABA *(things falling into place)* Ay – yay – yay... Does Murray know this? That your baby was with Brad?

ALICE Of course.

BABA Then why do you not marry Brad?

ALICE Well, we might well have married if his parents hadn't interfered, threatened to disinherit him.

BABA They did not approve of you?

ALICE What, him shacking up with a common little student working as a chambermaid? Shaven head, bright green lips, ring through her nose? No way. Still, he got his own back on them, didn't he – look who he married instead...

BABA But all the same you keep the baby?

ALICE They may have stopped Brad from marrying me but I wasn't giving that up as well. So his parents did the convenient thing instead. The way their sort always do. Tried to make it like it never happened. Paid us both off, Murray and me. Nice lump sum, convenient little cottage on their estate... It would have worked out fine if we'd both gone along with it. Me, I'd have taken the money and happily settled down...

BABA But Murray –?

ALICE I think in the end it was all a bit too dishonest for Murray. *(She smiles wryly)* That's what I like to think, anyway. But then again it could have been, after all that, he was no longer in love with me. Wouldn't have altogether blamed him... If only the bugger had warned me first. Instead of legging it at the last minute. Still. Mustn't complain. It was my own life I fucked up, wasn't it? That's the true version. Forget whatever he told you. Brad.

BABA Thank you. *(Looking at her, incredulously)* You had a ring through your nose? You? For real?

ALICE Still got the scar. I'll show you pictures of me sometime. In my day, I was glorious! Turned every head in that piddling little high street.

BABA We have a saying, too. *Assumasich noy licher.* Never leap to assumptions. Brad is not an honest man, I think. He is one of those – as you say – what's the bugger up to now? I am sorry for Kara sometimes. He is bad to her. He is telling her all the time she is a fool. Now the children are telling her the same. It is not good for her self-possession.

ALICE I wouldn't worry too much about that one if I were you, love, she's brighter than she looks. At least, I hope she is. No one can be that dopey.

BABA No, she's not dopey. Kara is my friend. I hope she is my friend still. Well thank you, Alice, I must now return to my trellis – no, to my trestle – table.

ALICE Just don't repeat what I've told you to Derek, will you?

BABA He does not know?

ALICE Derek's happier to see me as the victim. Brings out his protective side. You might bear that in mind with Murray.

BABA What? Me? I am no victim? Not at all.

ALICE No, but try to leave a tiny bit of you, dear, to let him know you still need him. Once he feels he's no longer needed, that he's surplus to requirements, he tends to piss off. Be warned. *(Attempting to rise)* I'll see you out.

BABA No, no please, don't bother...

ALICE No, that's alright, I can do with the – oh! Oh! Oh! *(She breaks off, as if having trouble with her breathing)* Oooh! Just a minute, I need to... Oh!

BABA *(concerned)* Alright?

ALICE Yes – I think – it'll pass – I have these occasionally... they tend to...

BABA *(stepping to support her)* Here – let me...

ALICE Oh, it's a bad one, this one! I don't think I can... Derek! I need Derek. Can you fetch Derek, please?

BABA Where is Derek? He's not here?

ALICE I don't know where he is. Find him! Quickly... Tell him I need him.

BABA *(steering her to the door)* Yes, you must lie down, Alice...

ALICE ...Quickly! Find him! Tell him I need him. I need Derek...

BABA *(as they leave)* Yes, I'll find him, don't worry. I'll find him...

As **BABA** *steers* **ALICE** *through the door, the lights cross fade to the living room.*

*   **BRAD** *comes trotting in from the garden. He is dressed in running kit, joggers and trainers. He has evidently been running some distance. Despite his exertion, he still seems reasonably fresh. He stops and looks back.*

BRAD *(calling back)* Come on, then! Where have you got to? Come on, keep up! Hup! Hup! Hup! Hup! ...

At last, **DEREK** *totters through the door, and throws himself down on a sofa. In his case, the unaccustomed exercise has definitely taken its toll.*

DEREK *(barely able to speak)* ...Jesus... I thought for a minute... I was going to die back there...

BRAD Pathetic! Look at you, you great Jessie.

DEREK *(breathless)* How long was...? How long was that, then?

BRAD Just under three miles, that.

DEREK Three miles? I don't normally <u>walk</u> three miles...

BRAD Well, you'd better start, sunbeam. Look at you, you're in a shocking state. I did warn you, didn't I? I told you to come prepared for a spot of exercise...

DEREK I didn't know you meant this sort of exercise, I thought you meant something gentler...on your putting green. Spot of table tennis...

BRAD Putting? Table tennis? You're no bloody use at those either, are you? You're useless.

DEREK Yes, I know that, I'm useless. You knew I was useless. Why ask me to run three miles? If you wanted someone to race with, you should have asked Murray. He'd have given you a race, Murray would.

BRAD *(frowning)* Yes. Well, another time. I must go and change. I'm due somewhere in an hour. Want a shower, do you? Not that you've even broken sweat, probably don't need one...

DEREK No thanks. A shower would probably wash me away... I couldn't cope with the force of the water...

BRAD *(shaking his head)* I don't know. Won't be a second. *(Stopping in the doorway)* Oh, by the way, yes. You owe me...

DEREK Owe you?

BRAD Five hundred quid...

DEREK Five hundr – oh, my God. You didn't –?

BRAD Piece of cake. Told you.

DEREK *(sotto, appalled)* With her? You didn't – with...her?

BRAD Push over. He doesn't win at everything, does he? Your precious hero? Don't worry, I'm happy to accept cash...

As he goes, he passes KARA *coming in.*

Oh, good morning darling. Got up at last, have you? Jolly good...

KARA I've been up for ages, Brad, you know that... What chance do I ever have for a lie in –? *(Seeing* DEREK*)* Oh, good morning, Derek. Didn't know you were here. That's nice. What brings you round at this time of morning?

DEREK 'Morning.

KARA You alright? You look terrible, if you don't mind me saying so... Dreadful.

DEREK Yes, well, Brad...he...he asked me to come for a run with him.

KARA A run? Where?

DEREK I don't know. Three miles somewhere, then back again...

KARA Three miles? Oh, Derek, you should be careful at your age... I mean, not that you're that old, but you read about men your age dropping dead, don't you?

DEREK I thought I had back there at one stage.

KARA Can I get you a cup of tea or something? Glass of water?

DEREK I'd appreciate a glass of water, Kara, thank you.

KARA Right. Won't be a moment. Wait there.

DEREK Thanks.

> **KARA** *goes out.* **DEREK** *studies his surroundings.* **BRAD** *enters, half changed but without his shirt.*

BRAD Kara, where the hell's my...? *(Looking round)* Where'd she go?

DEREK Gone to get me a glass of water. She's probably just in the –

BRAD *(irritably as he goes)* Stupid bloody woman...

> **BRAD** *goes out again.*

DEREK *(patting his chest, still in discomfort)* Oh, God! Slow down, slow down, you bugger...

> **KARA** *returns with a glass of water.*

KARA *(as she enters, to* BRAD*)* ...well, I didn't know you needed that one, did I? If you'd only said... *(Giving* DEREK *the glass)* What's he shouting at me for? He's got thousands of shirts, cupboards full of shirts... Here.

DEREK Thanks. *(He takes a grateful gulp)*

KARA It's out of the cooler. Should be nice and cold.

DEREK Perfect. That's better.

KARA You lose liquid when you're running.

DEREK I did. Halfway round, I had to have a piss behind a tree.

KARA Men are lucky like that. Don't have to bother, do they? Go anywhere, they can. Drop of a hat.

DEREK Hope not.

KARA Sorry?

DEREK Not in their hat.

KARA Oh, right. Yes.

They laugh. A slight pause.

Better than someone else's hat, anyway...

They both find this very amusing. Another slight pause.

Oh, it's good to have a laugh with someone now and again.

DEREK Do you not...do you not get many laughs then?

KARA *(guardedly)* Not...in the usual course of events, no. Not that many.

She seems rather subdued.

DEREK If you don't mind me saying so... I have to say this, Kara. He's sometimes not very nice to you, is he?

KARA What?

DEREK Your husband. Bordering on rude. He says terrible things to you sometimes, he really does.

KARA Does he?

DEREK You must have noticed, surely?

KARA Maybe I'm just used to them. I mean, I think when we first started out together, they were meant as sort of jokes. But as time went on... I mean, it does get me down occasionally, being called an idiot all day long, it's bound to... You begin to wonder whether it's true, eventually. But then I think, more fool me if I believe it, eh?

DEREK It concerns me, it really does.

KARA *(smiling at him)* Thank you, Derek. That's sweet of you, thank you. Whatever Brad says about you behind your back, you're a nice man.

DEREK Thank you.

A silence. They smile at each other.

This is a beautiful house, you know. I hadn't really properly taken it in before, you know. But... Lovely.

KARA Thank you. It's Brad's family home, of course. It's not that old, mind you, but... Brad's grandfather had it built. So it's been in the family three – no, coming up four generations, now...

DEREK But you've done things to it personally, since?

KARA Oh, yes. Masses. When I first moved in with Brad, it was that badly run down with just his mother living here. Then after she died, he gave me a free hand to do as I liked with it.

DEREK Left it to you, did he?

KARA Virtually. Too butch to choose nursery wall paper, was Brad. Woman's stuff, that was. Mind you, I did know a bit what I was doing. I was at art school way back. I was properly trained, briefly. And though I say it myself, I do have an eye. A natural eye. So I went ahead and indulged myself. Spent all his money. *(Smiling)* One of the benefits of being in this sort of prison. At least you get to decorate your own cell.

A silence.

Sorry, I didn't mean to say that. It came out wrong. Forget I said it.

DEREK You see this as a prison?

KARA Occasionally. I mean, I'm not complaining. As prisons go, it's paradise. But it's still a bloody prison, isn't it? Don't get me wrong, I'm perfectly free to come and go, of course I am. It's just – where the hell do I go?

DEREK You've got friends, though? You must have friends?

KARA Oh, yes. Mind you, they're mostly Brad's friends these days. Most of my friends have... In the early days, he sent most of the men packing, of course. He wasn't having competition. Not that sort, anyway. And as for my girl friends, they had to go as well...for their own slightly different reasons. I suppose I can always have a go at yoga or zumba classes or whatever. But what with the kids... I'm really pleased Baba's here. Hope she stays. I haven't known her long but I think she could become a real friend... We share a lot of the same interests...

DEREK *seems a little uncomfortable. He makes a further attempt to change the subject. At this point* BRAD, *fully changed, appears in the doorway. Unnoticed by them, he stops to listen.*

DEREK So how did you and Brad first meet, then? At a party, was it?

KARA *(evasive)* Yes. Yes, it was at a party, I suppose. Yes. I suppose you could call it a party, yes.

DEREK That's where most of us tended to meet, before the internet, wasn't it? At parties?

KARA Yes.

BRAD Mind you, it was a special sort of party, Derek.

KARA *and* DEREK *look up, startled.*

Tell him what sort of party it was, darling –

KARA Brad –

BRAD – go on, why don't you tell him –?

KARA – we were having a private conversation, Derek and I –

BRAD It was a stag party, Derek. Old Willy Mapleforth's stag do, wasn't it, darling? That's where we first met, wasn't it...?

KARA Brad, please, Derek doesn't want to know about that –

BRAD No, I'm sure he'll be fascinated, I'm sure he's curious to know what my lovely wife was doing at an all male stag do – Tell him.

KARA *(reluctantly)* I was there – as a – performance artist...

BRAD Now, you're being too modest, darling. You mustn't be so modest. The fact is Kara was the guest of honour, Derek.

KARA *(quietly)* Brad, please...

BRAD Now, what type of guest of honour would Kara be? At a stag party? Can you hazard a guess? Did she emerge from a cake, do you think? Any ideas, Derek? No? I'll tell you. Kara was what was known in those dissolute days as a strip-o-gram, Derek.

DEREK *(somewhat embarrassed)* Strip-o – Oh, I see...

KARA Brad, you promised you'd never –

BRAD Oh, come on, darling. Long, long ago now. You should have seen her, Derek. She was sensational. This ferocious looking policewoman stamped in, clad in full police regalia, and threatened to arrest poor Willy for indecent exposure on the Kingston bypass. And before the poor chap could say anything she'd whipped off her kit right down to her regulation police G string and she proceeds to give us the full works. I tell you, Derek, one glimpse of those independently whirling twin tassels and I said to myself, at last! At long last a woman I can safely take home to meet my mother! And the rest is history! It was literally love at first –

Derek, increasingly aware of Kara's discomfort, is no longer able to contain himself.

DEREK *(loudly and angrily)* Look, just shut the fuck up, would you, Brad! Can't you see that you're embarrassing her, man?

A silence.

BRAD *(coolly)* You'll have to excuse me. Late for my meeting. See you later, darling.

BRAD *goes out.*

A silence.

KARA *(stiffly)* I really must apologise for my husband, Derek, there was absolutely no need for that, none at all. I'm sorry if we embarrassed you.

DEREK No, no... *(Slight pause)* Did you really...?

KARA *(rather tight lipped)* Yes.

DEREK What, independently...? *(Gesturing vaguely)* You know...?

KARA It's not that difficult. Once you get the hang of it.

DEREK Right. I don't think I could do it... *(Coming to a decision)* Listen, Kara, about Brad. I have to tell you something about him. He and I, we both made a bet, you know...and...

KARA *(sharply)* A bet? What sort of bet?

DEREK Five hundred quid. He bet me he could...he could... you know –

The doorbell rings before he can finish. KARA *rises and moves to the door.*

KARA *(as she goes)* We'll talk about this in a minute, Derek. I need to hear more of this. Wait there...

She exits rapidly before DEREK *has a chance to speak.*

DEREK *(to the empty room)* Oh, God.

Voices off as **KARA** *answers the door.*

KARA *(offstage)* ...yes, he's just in here. He's sitting in there.

As **DEREK** *half rises,* **MURRAY** *comes in, followed closely by* **KARA.**

MURRAY *(as he enters)* Ah, Derek, mate, thank God I found you. I've just had Baba on the phone, she's at home with Alice... Now, there's no cause for alarm –

DEREK Alice, is she –

MURRAY – she's OK. But she's had another turn. Apparently she's had them before?

DEREK Yes, yes, she has, only –

MURRAY Now, it's just a precaution, just to be on the safe side, but they've sent for an ambulance...

DEREK Oh, my God, an ambulance...

MURRAY There's no need to worry, I'll run you up there...

DEREK *(as he goes out)* No, I've got my car just outside...oh, my God... Alice!

MURRAY *(following him)* Now, it's alright. Probably nothing serious... *(Turning back, briefly)* Oh, by the way, Kara, before I forget. Baba says she won't be able to baby-sit next week. She says very sorry but she's got that much on, at present...

KARA *(grimly)* Thank you, Murray. I fully understand. Tell her, when you see her, I fully understand. Tell her in those words, will you? That I fully understand.

MURRAY *goes out, looking a trifle puzzled by her tone of voice.* **KARA** *frowns. She hums to herself tunelessly, a sign of her inner agitation. She absently gathers up* **DEREK**'s *discarded glass. She stops and wriggles her torso, once or twice.*

(wincing, to herself) Oh, God, no. I couldn't do that now... no way!

As she goes, the lights cross fade to the kitchen. DEREK
enters, followed closely by MURRAY *who is holding his
mobile phone.*

MURRAY Baba's just texted...they're on their way there.

DEREK Right. I'll just collect up one or two of her things –

MURRAY Derek, there's no hurry, mate, she's in good hands...
Catch your breath a minute. No, really. They'll be checking
her over first. Probably won't even let you in to see her.
Relax, man.

*The model train arrives and goes through its usual
ritual. Both watch it for a moment.*

MURRAY *wanders to the window.* DEREK *does his best
to relax but remains on edge.*

Great view of the hotel from here...

DEREK Oh, yes. Alice stands there, staring at it for ages. I say to
her, what are you doing, waiting for it to fall down, are you?

MURRAY Just look at them all. Baba's volunteer army down
there, manning the trestles. She's certainly got things
organised...

DEREK Listen, you don't have to come with me if you'd rather...

MURRAY No, I'm happy to come. You need a friend, don't you?
Time like this?

DEREK *(touched by this)* Yes, I do. I do need a friend. Thanks,
Murray. Listen, as a friend – do you mind me saying to you,
keep her close, won't you?

MURRAY Close? Who, Baba? How do you mean, close?

DEREK Just don't – let her stray too far away from you... Know
what I mean?

MURRAY No idea what you're talking about, mate. Have you
heard something?

DEREK Oh, nothing. Just rumours...

MURRAY You must have heard something...

DEREK *(making to leave)* Look, forget it. I must go. I need to be with Alice. I know what's she's like...

MURRAY *(following him out)* No, wait, what have you heard, Derek...?

They go off.

DEREK *(offstage)* She'll need me there or she'll fret, I know her...

MURRAY *(offstage)* Derek!

As their voices recede, the lights cross fade back to the living room.

*The sounds of gunshots from the garden as **KARA** comes on from the house. She crosses to the garden door. Waiting for a pause in the shots, she calls out as if not for the first time.*

KARA *(calling, wearily)* Brad...please... Come on, that's enough... Brad! <u>Please!</u>

*One or two more shots. In a moment, **BRAD** appears, broken open gun in hand.*

BRAD What? What do you want?

KARA It's half past nine. Do you have to keep making that din...?

BRAD We're hardly going to get complaints from the neighbours, darling, are we? They're miles away.

KARA It's not the neighbours, Brad, it's us. Me and the kids. What's the matter with you? It's pitch dark out there.

BRAD No, it isn't. I've got the lights on.

He props the gun against a chair and goes to pour himself a scotch during the next.

KARA What lights?

BRAD The security lights. I've over-ridden the sensors. It's like daylight back there...

KARA You're obsessed with that thing...that machine...

BRAD *(offering a drink)* Want one...?

KARA *(mildly irritated)* No, I don't want one. I certainly don't want one now. You're obsessed with that machine, aren't you? Ever since –

BRAD Ever since what?

KARA Ever since Murray beat you on it. You hate losing, don't you? You can't bear it if someone beats you...

BRAD Can't help it, darling, it's genetic. It's a man thing. Men hate to lose. It's the nature of the male species. The competitive gene. My father was competitive – Christ, was he competitive – I take after him. And, mark my words, when he grows up, young Billy will be exactly the same –

KARA Not if I can help it, he won't.

BRAD Want to bet? *(He sips his drink)*

KARA Anyway, it doesn't necessarily follow. Not all men are competitive. I know plenty of men that aren't.

BRAD Name three.

KARA Well, Derek for one. Derek's not competitive, is he?

BRAD Underneath he is. Probably even more so than I am. It's simply that Derek's one of those who's chosen to opt out. But deep down he's sitting there on the reserve benches simply itching to take part. Desperate to. But his sort, they're so fucking terrified of losing, they haven't even got the guts to take part. He's a sad, pathetic little shit and he's no longer welcome in this house, I can tell you that.

KARA Oh, dear. Because he stood up for me? That the reason?

BRAD *scowls but does not reply.*

I could beat you, you know.

BRAD *(startled)* What?

KARA I said, I could beat you. At shooting. I could. I'm a far better shot than you'll ever be.

BRAD *(amused)* You must be joking. You don't even like guns, you're terrified of them. You're like a scared mouse, soon as you go near them...

KARA I could still beat you. Bet you I could.

BRAD Nonsense. *(He stares at her)* You're serious, aren't you?

KARA Deadly serious.

BRAD The mouse showing its tiny claws at last! Squeak! Squeak! I rather like you when you're in your Joan of Arc mood, darling. Alright, you're on. How much do you want to bet?

KARA *(fractional pause)* Five hundred quid.

BRAD *(rising)* Done. You're on.

KARA *(moving)* I'll fetch another gun.

BRAD What, now? You want to do it right now?

KARA Why not? While I'm in the mood, why not?

> **KARA** *goes out.*

BRAD *(amused, to himself)* Absolutely bonkers. Brain the size of a pea...

> *He pours himself another scotch.*

> **KARA** *returns with a gun.*

KARA Right. Ready, then?

BRAD Have you checked it?

KARA How do you mean?

BRAD First rule of a gun, dumbo! Before you first pick it up, you check it isn't loaded. Then, when you finally put it down, you do the same. You check it! So have you checked it? You've checked it isn't loaded?

KARA Yes, I've checked it.

BRAD *(draining his glass)* This is completely crazy, you know. Look at you, you can hardly lift the bloody thing. Pathetic. You're going to make an utter fool of yourself, you know that. Come on, then.

BRAD moves to the garden door. KARA follows him.

(as they go out) Now, for God's sake keep it pointing at the ground, girl. We don't want any idiotic accidents, do we? I don't relish carting you up to A&E because you've blown your foot off. *(Offstage, angrily)* And don't point the thing at me either, you daft woman! How many more times do I need to tell you, you silly –

A loud gunshot. Quite close this time.

A silence. A cry from BRAD, half in shock, half in pain.

(his dying words) – stupid – bitch...!

KARA comes back into the room without her gun. She appears in shock.

KARA *(stunned, quietly)* Oh, God! Oh, my God! *(Growing slightly more hysterical)* Oh, God! Oh, God! Oh, God! Oh, God!

From upstairs, the sound of a child's voice.

DAISY *(her voice, offstage)* Mum? What's happening? Mum?

KARA *(calling)* It's alright, darling! Go back to bed! It's alright!

DAISY *(her voice, offstage)* Mum?

KARA No, don't come! You stay up there. Nothing to worry about. Daddy's – daddy's just had a slight accident, that's all!

KARA *stands, as if torn between which course of action to take, returning to* BRAD *or seeing to her children. In the end, she hurries off upstairs, the lights fade to blackout.*

End of Act II Scene One

Scene Two

A day or two later.

The lights come up on the bedroom where **BABA** *is sitting, looking serious and studying her dictionary.*

Lower level lights in the kitchen on **DEREK**, *sitting at the table. He is busy painting a model railway station. He too appears preoccupied.*

BABA *(reading softly)* ...con – dol – en – ces...com – mis – erations. My deep – sympathy – for your loss... *(Practising a few off the cuff)* How sad! How simply awful for you! I'm so sorry. Sorry! Sorry! *(She shrugs and gives up)*

BABA *puts the book down on the dressing table and goes out. The lights fade down on the bedroom.*

In the kitchen, another train arrives, stops for the signal, toots merrily and proceeds on its way. **DEREK** *checks his watch, appears satisfied and continues with his delicate task. The doorbell rings. He rises, still abstracted, and goes to answer it.*

In a moment, he returns with **MURRAY**.

MURRAY *(as they enter)* Sorry to disturb you, mate. I know you must have plenty of worries of your own, what with one thing and another. But I just couldn't sleep last night. I had to talk to someone...

DEREK No, I've been the same, what with... Any further news, then?

MURRAY No, well, apparently one of the kids phoned the ambulance – Kara was hysterical – by the time it got there – Brad was declared dead – he took it full in the chest. Point blank range...

DEREK *(wincing)* Oooh...

MURRAY The police were called. Declared it a crime scene. Then in due course, once they'd calmed her down, they took Kara in for questioning.

DEREK She's not... I mean, the police don't think – do they? That Kara –? They can't, surely? She hated guns, she couldn't stand them.

MURRAY Guns are guns, aren't they? What was it my old sergeant used to say? You don't have to love 'em, lad, to fire 'em. Tell me, how's Alice?

DEREK Still in there. I go up to visit regularly, of course. It was quite a severe one, more serious than they first thought. She's lost all her speech now. Most of her movement. It's just so – Thirty-nine, you know, that's all she is. I need to get her home. The sooner the better. For both of us.

MURRAY Ah. What's that you're doing?

DEREK New station, see? North Lounge.

MURRAY North Lounge?

DEREK Yes, I've got a South Lounge already.

MURRAY How many stations have you got, then?

DEREK Oh, now...let me see... I keep adding to them... There's – let's see – *(Counting on his fingers)* South Lounge – soon as this is finished – North Lounge – North Hall, South Hall, West Dining Room, East Dining Room, Toilet –

MURRAY Toilet? You got trains running through your toilet?

DEREK Just the guest toilet, you know. Not the en suite. Alice drew the line at that –

MURRAY I bet she did...

DEREK I'll show you round later, if you like...a guided tour.

MURRAY No, well, maybe another time, Derek...

DEREK Well, you must see my masterpiece, anyway –

MURRAY Masterpiece?

DEREK Where it all started. Nursery Grand Central.

MURRAY Nursery? You got a nursery?

DEREK Yes, while Alice was expecting, you know, we first got married, after we moved in here, I decorated the spare room for him – for Toby – we called him Toby, you know – I decorated it as a nursery, you know. Then a month or so after he was born, while Toby was still small, before we discovered he had – I bought him this little train set. Just a small circle, like, one goods engine, couple of trucks – thought it might keep him amused, watching it going round and round. *(Laughing)* Certainly kept me amused, anyway. Alice said, come on, you just bought it for you, didn't you? Not for Toby at all! And then, of course, we found out, you know, that things weren't quite right with him – something wrong – I think these days they could have dealt with it, no problem... Still. There you go – So, after that, the layout's just grown and grown. Over the years. I like to think sometimes, wherever he is, Toby, you know, he'll still be watching his trains going round. Somewhere. Wherever he is. Probably not. Daft.

MURRAY *(gently)* No, it's not daft. Not daft at all.

They both stare at the station for a moment.

Derek, listen, the reason I came round... What you said to me the other day about Baba – keeping her close –

DEREK No, I shouldn't have said anything. Out of order. Forget about it. Sorry.

MURRAY No, you can't leave it like that, mate. You have to tell me the rest, Derek, you owe me that...

DEREK Sorry. My lips are sealed, Murray. I'm not saying a further word. I don't intend to speak ill of the dead, I – *(Realising he's said too much)* – oh!

MURRAY So it is to do with her and Brad, then?

DEREK Ah. You guessed...

MURRAY I knew it had to be. I knew it... I'd go round there and throttle him, only now the bugger's dead, what'd be the point? What did he tell you? He told you something, didn't he? He must have done.

DEREK He... He and I, we... God, I'm not at all proud of this, Murray, I'm really not. In fact if you must know, I'm really ashamed of myself – we...we...he and I, we –

MURRAY What? What did you do, you two?

DEREK We made a sort of bet.

MURRAY What sort of bet?

DEREK I didn't want to. It was his idea. All his... But you know Brad with his bets, you know what he's like – what he <u>was</u> like...

MURRAY What was it he bet you?

DEREK He bet me he could – God, I'm so ashamed of this, you've no idea – Brad bet me that he could take Baba off you within two weeks. You know, have her. Get her into bed. I said to him, no way, she's a wonderful loyal wife, you can tell that just from looking –

MURRAY *(grimly)* How much was the bet for?

DEREK – I said to him, Brad, mate just look at her! Did you ever see a more –?

MURRAY *(quietly)* How much was the bet for, Derek?

DEREK *(in a small voice)* Five hundred quid.

MURRAY Five hundred? You and him were betting on my wife's virtue, her integrity, for five hundred quid? Five hundred bloody pieces of silver, Derek?

DEREK Well, it started out at a thousand but I told him, no way I'm taking your money, mate. No way...

MURRAY You were happy to take five hundred off him, though...?

DEREK Well, I would have been. For five hundred I would have been, only...

MURRAY Only? *(A pause)* Only what?

DEREK Only I lost.

Another silence while **MURRAY** *digests this.*

MURRAY You lost?

DEREK I lost the bet.

MURRAY You mean Brad won?

DEREK Yes.

MURRAY How do you know he won?

DEREK Well, he told me.

MURRAY When did he tell you?

DEREK Yesterday.

> **MURRAY** *rises and stares out of the window.*

> **DEREK** *watches him nervously.*

But then you know Brad – you knew Brad. What he's like. Was like. He could just as well have been lying, couldn't he? Brad would always cheat, given half the chance, wouldn't he? *(Tentatively)* Do you think that's possibly the reason, then? Why Kara might possibly have shot him? On account of him having...? Brad having...?

MURRAY *(grimly)* Possibly. Saved me the job, anyway.

DEREK What you going to do now, Murray?

MURRAY I don't know. I've really no idea. I'm in that much of a state at the moment, Derek, there's no knowing what I'll do... Apart from extending your railway by using your arse for a tunnel, I'm totally devoid of ideas. Goodbye, then. *(He moves to the door)*

DEREK *(as he goes)* Murray, don't do anything rash now, will you? Don't do anything stupid, will you?

> **MURRAY** *goes out.*

(to himself, worriedly) I do hope he doesn't do anything stupid...

After a second, he gathers up his model and materials and goes off. As this happens, the lights cross fade to the living room.

BABA *enters and looks around.*

BABA *(calling)* Hallo...hallo...? Is someone here, please?

She moves to the garden windows and looks out.

Oh.

After a second, **SIMONE (SIMMY)** *enters. She is seventeen years old and looks very like her mother,* **KARA**. *Seeing* **BABA**, *she frowns.*

SIMMY *(coolly)* Can I help you at all?

BABA Yes, I – *(Seeing* **SIMMY**, *confused)* Oh –

SIMMY Can I help you?

BABA You are –? Oh, yes, of course, you're Simmy –?

SIMMY Simone, yes...

BABA For a minute I thought – I'm sorry, the front door was open –

SIMMY Yes, probably the crime scene people. They're in and out all day –

BABA Yes, I see they are out there still investigating. That is where –? Where he –? She –? Of course you're Simone. You are so like – like your –

SIMMY *(brusquely)* Like my mother? Yes, so I'm told. What are you doing here? What do you want?

BABA I came round to say – I wanted to see Kara. I wanted to talk to your mother...

SIMMY Well, you can't. She's still at the police station. Under suspicion of murdering my father. So you can't. I repeat, what can I do for you?

BABA I wanted to say – I'm sorry...how sorry I am...

SIMMY Bit late for that really, isn't it?

BABA What?

SIMMY Bit late for sorry, isn't it? To come round here and say you're sorry? What good's that going to do now?

BABA *(confused)* I'm sorry?

SIMMY *(angrily)* Don't keep saying it. Sorry, sorry, sorry... You don't even mean it, do you? You befriend my mother, who trusted you, was stupid enough to think of you as her friend... She really liked you, you know? Really rated you. Then what do you do, in return? You fuck my father practically in front of my kid brother and sister – and all you can say is "I'm sorry"...

BABA *(bewildered)* Fuck? What is this, fuck your father...?

SIMMY Now, just get out...

BABA ...why are you being antagonistic to me? We did not fuck...

SIMMY ...I'm not going to tell you again...

BABA ...there was no fuck, no, I'm so sorry...

SIMMY Will you stop saying you're fucking sorry...now, get out of this house...

BABA ...I swear we did not fuck, Simmy, I swear it!

SIMMY If you don't leave now, I'll get the police out there to throw you out...the place is crawling with them, thanks to you...

BABA *(retreating, tearfully)* ...Simmy, there was no fuck, I swear... I'm so sorry... There is no cause for us to be acrimonious...

SIMMY *(driving BABA through the doorway, angrily)* If there was any justice, it's you they should threaten with prison, not her... I've seen you there in the precinct, handing out your tacky little leaflets, trying to save your grimy little pub. Well, I tell you, nobody wants you here, either of you, you can both fuck off back to where you came from, alright?

BABA *(offstage, as she goes, distressed)* Sorry, I'm sorry, I'm so, so sorry...

> BABA *goes out.* SIMMY *watches her leave, then recovers, aware the proceedings are being watched from outside through the window. She moves to the garden door.*

SIMMY *(calling, through the glass, smiling)* It's alright. Just some loony, it's alright! Carry on, officers! *(She gives them a cod salute) (Under her breath)* Arseholes!

> *She returns and goes back to the house. As she does so, the lights cross fade to the bedroom.*

> MURRAY *enters. He has his coat on and is carrying his holdall, presumably containing all his worldly possessions. He stands, slowly taking in the room for a final time. He picks up the dictionary which* BABA *has left on the dressing table. He appears to be on the verge of tears. He replaces the book and with fresh determination he exits swiftly.*

> *In the kitchen,* DEREK *has re-entered. He is carrying a small recording device which he sets up on the table. He takes a notebook from his pocket. He opens it and silently mouthing, rehearses first. He then sets the recorder running.*

DEREK *(holding his nose and speaking into his hand)* This is Kitchen! This is Kitchen. The train now standing at platform 1 is the stopping train to Nursery, calling at South Hall, North Hall and all stations to Nursery.

> *He stops the machine and plays back the result.*

(satisfied) That's good. That's brilliant! That'll do... *(Looking at his watch, suddenly aware of the time)* Oh, no! Look at the time...

DEREK *gathers up his stuff and hurries out again.*

In the bedroom, **BABA** *enters.*

BABA *(puzzled)* Murray? *(She listens)* Murray? You here? Murray?

She goes out again.

(offstage) Murray? *Wisser iss?*

She returns almost immediately.

Oh, God! *Alla evarneen! Evarneen!* All of him is gone! All of him! Where's he go! *(With a little cry)* Murray! Murray! You can't go! *Nargich! Nargich!* You can't go!

She sits on the bed, confused and miserable, shivering slightly.

Lights come up on the kitchen, as **DEREK** *enters, pushing* **ALICE** *in a wheelchair. She is unable to speak and seems very frail.*

DEREK Here we are, my love, home again. That's better, isn't it? It's a lot nicer, to be home, isn't it? Nothing's changed, I promise. All just the same. Well, one or two improvements in the railway department. Some new surprises for you. Just wait and hear what I've been up to. You have a listen. I'll just go and turn the bed down, switch on the blanket, make sure everything's ready for you... Won't be long. You wait in here till the next train arrives. There's one duc in a moment. Have a listen!

DEREK *goes out again leaving* **ALICE** *parked in the kitchen.*

In the bedroom, **BABA** *has not moved.*

BABA *(wailing like a child)* Murray! Murray! MURRAY!

She rises and moves to the dressing table. She is evidently in mid panic attack. She takes her container of tablets from the drawer and struggles with the lid.

(in increasing frustration) Bizzelpurken! Oh, damn you! Bother you! Piss! Bollocks! Buggery! Thing!

She throws down the container in fury and sits on the bed and curls up into a ball.

(muffled, in a small voice) Murray! Murray! Where you gone, Murray? Where you gone, you bugger? Where you gone?

In the kitchen, **ALICE** *remains silently in her wheelchair. The model train approaches and stops.*

Tiny voices from a loudspeaker hidden somewhere are heard. **DEREK** *has clearly recorded all the voices himself.*

ALICE *listens to this incredulously.*

ANNCR This is Kitchen! This is Kitchen. Next stop South Hall. This is the Nursery train, calling at all stations to Nursery.

VOICE 1 *(cheerily)* Come on kids, hurry up! All aboard, now! We don't want it to go without us now, do we?

VOICE 2 Oh, Daddy, wait, wait...

VOICE 1 Come on, up you climb, Timmy! Hup! Safe aboard now, Sally?

VOICE 3 Yes, Daddy.

VOICE 1 Julie?

VOICE 4 Yes, Daddy.

VOICE 1 Then, off we go then! Hold tight!

The train whistles and moves away. **ALICE** *makes a muffled groaning sound and raises her eyes to heaven.*

In the bedroom, **BABA** *has curled up and fallen asleep.* **MURRAY** *enters quietly. He is very subdued. He watches her.* **BABA** *wakes up suddenly, as if by instinct.*

BABA *(staring at him)* Murray?

MURRAY *(muted, rather sheepishly)* Hallo.

BABA I thought you'd gone. I thought you'd left…

MURRAY Yes, well I was, half way to going…and I thought… no, not again… I can't walk out again, not a second time.

BABA No, that's not good. Why? Why, Murray? Why did you want to?

MURRAY Don't know. It just seemed suddenly to get – all too much – you know, same as it was the last time –

BABA The last time?

MURRAY Last time I left. The last time I walked away. Seemed for a minute, it was all happening again…history repeating itself, you know. Me, messing things up. Again. After all I'd promised you…and then what with you losing confidence in me. With Brad…

BABA Brad?

MURRAY Yes, I know all that. Derek told me…about you and Brad.

BABA Me and Brad? No, there was never me and Brad. Never. Who told you this? Derek? Me and Brad? It is a concoction! A ridiculous fabrication! Why is everyone saying this? First it is Simmy. Now you. What is this? Murray, I swear to God and on my grandmother's grave – I never ever fuck with Brad.

MURRAY It's not true?

BABA No! Why did not you ask me before? I'm an honest woman, Murray. I tell you if I fuck. I tell you, honestly. You don't trust me?

MURRAY Yes. I trust you, Baba. Course I do. It's just – I don't know – if I'd asked you, straight out, like, you might have thought I was – you know – it sounds daft but – I thought you might think I was accusing you. I was afraid you'd accuse me of accusing you, you know...

BABA Accuse you of – this is ridiculous, I don't understand this stupid language at all. It is nonsensical. Why didn't you simply ask me, Murray? Baba, did you fuck or did you not fuck? Yes or no?

MURRAY *(distressed)* Because I was terrified you'd say "Yes, I did"! That's why!

A silence.

BABA *(tenderly)* Oh, my dear, oh my! For a hero, there is so much that terrifies you, isn't there, my darling?

MURRAY Not even that much of a hero, either. Most of that's a lie as well...

BABA It's not true?

MURRAY Not really.

BABA None of it? How did you get your medal, then, if it was not true?

MURRAY Oh, it was true. Partly. True we were under fire from these snipers. And I did climb the scaffolding outside this children's hospital. And I brought it down, it collapsed, and these two snipers were killed in the fall. That was all true. Only when we turned them over to examine them, you know, to make sure they were both dead – we found they were only kids.

BABA Kids?

MURRAY You know, thirteen, fourteen year olds. Maybe as young as twelve, I don't know. And then when we got inside the building and exchanged further fire – self defence really – when that was all over, it turned out they were kids, we'd been fighting kids as well. Not a single adult left in the place. The medical staff had all buggered off, most of them,

the ones their lot hadn't massacred. The kids were told to
hold the fort.

BABA And the ones you rescued, the little ones?

MURRAY The ones hiding in the basement? They weren't locked
in at all, they were just hiding. From us. Soon as they heard
we were inside the building, they hid.

BABA And they set fire to it, the small children?

MURRAY No, I think that was us. During the fire fight, we
must have hit something. It might have even been me, I
don't know, there was that much stuff flying about. Ironic
that, eh? There I was gallantly rescuing kids from a fire I
possibly helped to start. They were screaming but it wasn't
the fire they were terrified of. It was us. They'd been told,
if we got hold of them, us lot, we'd eat them alive.

BABA Grown-ups love to tell small children stories to frighten
them. When I was small my grandmother said if I told lies
to those who loved me, my tongue would grow black and
fall out from my head...

MURRAY She sounds a bit like my granddad. So, anyway, after
it's all over, while I was in hospital, recovering, this bloke
comes in to see me, this major. Never seen him before or
since. Told me they were considering me for a medal. Only
he said, 'We may have to just doctor the facts slightly, old
chap' – those were his words. Only if the story got out that
we'd actually been shooting at a bunch of kids, even killing
some of them...well, that wouldn't go down quite so good,
would it? Bad for morale. For the image, back home. Might
lose a bit of public support for the war. So there you have
it. That's the true story. Some bloody hero, eh?

BABA You still rescued the small children. You still risked your
life for them from the fire which you may or may not have
started. And you didn't eat them alive. (*Holding out her
arms*) So for me, my darling, you are still my hero.

MURRAY *comes and sits beside her. She draws him down
so his head rests in her lap.*

(kissing him gently) You don't always have to be a hero for me, not all the time. Sometimes it's possible I can be a hero, too. We take turns.

MURRAY I do love you, Baba. I really do. You don't mind me calling you Baba, do you?

BABA No, no. You, I don't mind. That is your name for me. Other people, they must call me by my proper name. Madrababacascabuna. I will insist.

MURRAY Difficult for most people. One hell of a mouthful.

BABA Yes, it is. One hell of a mouthful. Hard cheese for them.

MURRAY *(amused)* You still love me, Baba, don't you?

BABA Oh, yes. I still love you. I love you most because you are...?

MURRAY I'm good looking...?

BABA No, no, no. I don't love you just for good looking...yes, you are good looking but not only for that – I love you because...

MURRAY I'm witty? Dashing? Brave?

BABA No. I love you because you are – idiosyncratic...

MURRAY Bloody hell! What's that mean?

BABA It means you are you. Because you are you. You are no one else. But you.

In the kitchen, DEREK *returns for* ALICE.

DEREK You set? It's all ready for you. Here we go. *(As they go)* Did you hear the train in the station, by the way? Bet that was a surprise for you, wasn't it? I've recorded masses more. I plan to record a little bit for every station. Isn't that a great idea?

ALICE *makes another sound.*

They go out. Back in the bedroom, BABA *and* MURRAY *haven't shifted their position.*

BABA *(stroking his hair)* You know, we have over five hundred signatures. 'Save The Bird of Prey – An endangered species'. They will need to listen. I am determined. We will win, my darling. Trust me. I am strong. And if we lose – then there will be other things, never fear. Don't be afraid, my darling, don't be frightened... Murray?

MURRAY has fallen asleep in her lap. She kisses him gently.

(whispering softly in his ear) I'm here. I will be your hero.

The lights fade up on the living room. SIMMY enters in her boiler suit. She is slightly smoke blackened and carries an empty petrol can which she tosses down.

SIMMY *(in quiet triumph)* Yes!!!

She goes to the sideboard and takes out the bottle of single malt. She contemplates pouring a glass then decides to drink it straight from the bottle. She sits on the sofa, still holding the bottle.

Meanwhile back in the bedroom, a distant fire engine races past. Both occupants, now asleep, fail to notice it.

In the kitchen, the first signs of flames from the precinct opposite are beginning to be reflected in the room. A fire engine, very much louder, arrives outside. The sounds of the crew starting to tackle the blaze can be heard. DEREK enters in his dressing gown. He looks out of the window.

DEREK *(alarmed)* Oh, no! Alice! Alice love...oh, no...the whole place is on fire! Alice! You'll have to get up again, love...

DEREK hurries out.

In the bedroom, another fire engine passes, this time waking MURRAY. He rises, careful not to wake BABA, and crosses to the window. His face is faintly lit by the fire some half a mile away.

SIMMY rises and also goes to her own window. Her face is also lit, though even more dimly, from the fire over two miles away. She raises the bottle, in an ironic toast.

In the kitchen, DEREK enters, pushing ALICE in her wheelchair. She is now also in her dressing gown. They move to their window. The fire is much brighter here and the sounds of activity down in the precinct increase. In the bedroom, BABA wakes up and sees MURRAY by the window.

Music starts under the next.

BABA What is it, darling?

MURRAY Big fire somewhere. Right in the town centre from the look of it... Oh!

They look at each other, as the possibility of what it might be occurs to both of them.

BABA moves to him and hugs him.

BABA Don't be afraid. Heroes together, yes?

MURRAY Yes. Heroes together!

The final image of all of them at their respective windows watching the fire at its various intensities. The sounds of the activity outside in the precinct increases.

As the music builds, the lights fade to:

Blackout.

PROPS

ACT ONE
Two sofas - one permanent fixture in the Living Room, one temporary seating for the TV Studio set-up. (p1)
Mobile tablet (p1)
Table (p1)
Two stools (p1)
Visible part of an extensive model railway – the bit that can be seen is a tunnel to a small station. The line then continues on, stops briefly at a set of operating signals, currently at red and, as they turn green, finally disappears into another stretch of tunnel (p1)
Cup of Coffee (p1)
Two TV Remotes - for Alice and Kara (p7)
Broken-open shotgun (p7)
Baba: carrying her dress (p9)
English phrasebook (p9)
Dressing table with make-up on (p9)
Derek: dressed in male consort chain, carrying the Mayor's chain (p9)
Model electric train (p9)
Screwtop container of tablets (p13)
Sideboard cupboard (p25)
Single malt whisky (p25)
Glass (p25)
Bed (p28)
Dictionary (p28)
Modest sized glass of brandy (p28)
Bag (p48)
Exercise book (p48)
Small English dictionary (p48)
Two glasses (p49)

ACT TWO

Glass of water (p64)
Mobile phone (p71)
Another gun (p74)
A part-painted model railway station, paints and brushes (p77)
Holdall (p84)
A small recording device (p84)
Wheelchair (p85)
Empty petrol can (p91)

LIGHTING

ACT ONE

House lights fade to black out (p1)
Lights come up (p1)
Lights snap out on Murray and Baba (p7)
Lights cross fade to living room (p13)
Lights cross fade to kitchen (p23)
Lights come up on the bedroom (p27)
Lights fade on all areas (p29)
The lights come up on the living room (p30)
Lights cross fade to the kitchen (p40)
Lights cross fade back to the living room (p44)
Lights cross fade back to the kitchen (p45)
Lights cross fade back to the living room (p48)
Lights cross fade to the bedroom (p55)
Lights fade to blackout (p56)

ACT TWO

Lights cross fade to the living room (p62)
Lights cross fade to the kitchen (p71)
Lights cross fade to the living room (p72)
Lights fade to blackout (p76)
Lights come up on the bedroom and a lower level light on Derek in the kitchen (p77)
Lights fade down on the bedroom (p77)

Lights cross fade to the living room (p82)
Lights cross fade to the bedroom (p84)
Lights come up in the kitchen (p85)
Lights fade up on living room (p91)
In the kitchen, the first signs of flames from the precinct opposite (p91)
Murray's face is faintly lit by the fire (p91)
Simmy's face is also lit, more dimly (p92)
The fire is much brighter through the window into Alice and Derek's kitchen (p92)
Lights fade (p92)
Blackout (p92)

SOUND EFFECTS

ACT ONE
Sounds of a triumphal parades with a band (p1)
Doorbell rings (p16)
Doorbell rings (p19)
Murmur of the waiting room (p23)
Town band strikes up a fanfare (p23)
Sound fades (p23)
Shotgun blasts – clay pigeon shooting (p30)
A burst of gunfire (p31)
More gunfire (p32)
Rapping on the garden door (p48)
Music starts under (p56)

ACT TWO
Doorbell rings (p69)
Sound of gunshots (p72)
A loud gunshot (p75)
Doorbell rings (p77)
Tiny voices from a loudspeaker are heard (p86)
Playback from small recording device (p84)
Fire engine, louder as it arrives, and sounds of crew tackling the blaze (p91)
Another fire engine passes (p91)

Sound of activity in the precinct increases (p92)

ADDITIONAL NOTE: MODEL TRAIN CUES

The model train and the station / lights operate on the following cues:

Model train comes out of the tunnel and stops briefly at the station (p9)
As the lights turn green, the train whistles and moves on (p9)
The model train emerges once again from its tunnel in the kitchen. It stops briefly at the station, sounds its whistle and, once the signal turns green, proceeds on its way, as before (p29)
The model train passes again, giving its familiar cheery whistle (p44)
The train arrives at the station and goes through its routine (p47)
The model train arrives and goes through its usual ritual (p71)
In the kitchen, another train arrives, stops for the signal, toots merrily and proceeds on its way (p77)
The model train approaches and stops (p86)
The train whistles and moves away (p86)

VISIT THE
SAMUEL FRENCH
BOOKSHOP
AT THE
ROYAL COURT THEATRE

Browse plays and theatre books, get expert advice and enjoy a coffee

Samuel French Bookshop
Royal Court Theatre
Sloane Square
London
SW1W 8AS
020 7565 5024

Shop from thousands of titles on our website

 samuelfrench.co.uk

 samuelfrenchltd

 samuel french uk

Lightning Source UK Ltd.
Milton Keynes UK
UKHW020642080219
336934UK00013B/2206/P

9 780573 112201